T0383073

# Cultural and Sociological Aspects of Alcoholism and Substance Abuse

The *Advances in Alcohol & Substance Abuse* series:

- *Opiate Receptors, Neurotransmitters, & Drug Dependence: Basic Science-Clinical Correlates*
- *Recent Advances in the Biology of Alcoholism*
- *The Effects of Maternal Alcohol and Drug Abuse on the Newborn*
- *Evaluation of Drug Treatment Programs*
- *Current Controversies in Alcoholism*
- *Federal Priorities in Funding Alcohol and Drug Abuse Programs*
- *Psychosocial Constructs of Alcoholism and Substance Abuse*
- *The Addictive Behaviors*
- *Conceptual Issues in Alcoholism and Substance Abuse*
- *Dual Addiction: Pharmacological Issues in the Treatment of Concomitant Alcoholism and Drug Abuse*
- *Cultural and Sociological Aspects of Alcoholism and Substance Abuse*
- *Alcohol and Drug Abuse in the Affluent*
- *Alcohol and Substance Abuse in Adolescence*

# Cultural and Sociological Aspects of Alcoholism and Substance Abuse

Barry Stimmel, MD, Editor

The Haworth Press
New York

*Cultural and Sociological Aspects of Alcoholism and Substance Abuse* has also been published as *Advances in Alcohol & Substance Abuse,* Volume 4, Number 1, Fall 1984.

Reprint 2007
The Haworth Press, Inc., 10 Alice Street, Binghamton, NY 13904-1580

**Library of Congress Cataloging in Publication Data**
Main entry under title:

Cultural and sociological aspects of alcoholism
    and substance abuse.

    Published also as v. 4, no. 1, Fall 1984 of the Advances in alcohol & substance
abuse.
    Includes bibliographies.
    1. Substance abuse—United States—Addresses, essays, lectures. 2. Alco-
holism—United States—Addresses, essays, lectures. I. Stimmel, Barry, 1939- .
HV4999.2.C84 1984      362.2'92'0973      84-12985
ISBN 0-86656-367-9

# Cultural and Sociological Aspects of Alcoholism and Substance Abuse

Advances in Alcohol & Substance Abuse
Volume 4, Number 1

## CONTENTS

## SELECTIVE GUIDE TO CURRENT REFERENCE SOURCES ON TOPICS DISCUSSED IN THIS ISSUE

# Cultural and Sociological Aspects of Alcoholism and Substance Abuse

# EDITORIAL

# The Role of Ethnography
# in Alcoholism and Substance Abuse:
# The Nature versus Nurture Controversy

Although a knowledge of the pharmacologic effects of mood-altering drugs and the medical complications associated with their use is essential to provide adequate therapy, the importance of identifying causal factors related to their use cannot be overemphasized. The cultural and psychosocial aspects of alcoholism and substance abuse are studied most often through ethnography. Ethnography can best be described as an analysis of behaviors that characterize and distinguish cultures or sociocultural groups.[1] Such groups may represent macrocultures or subcultures, including family units. Much of the epidemiological data pertaining to substance abuse comes from ethnographers through first-hand observations and interviews. This issue of *Advances* focuses on selected aspects of the sociocultural interactions between alcoholism and substance abuse.

Westermeyer, in the lead paper, reviews the role of ethnicity in substance abuse, as well as the limitations inherent in relying solely upon this technique.[2] Ethnography, while providing essential information, fails, unfortunately, to provide controls to test specific hypotheses and may unintentionally detract from relevant biologic factors of equal or greater importance. When one reviews the multiple factors implicated in the development of a chemical dependency, the identification of those consistently found to be relevant seems overwhelming. For example, it has long been recognized that the prevalence of heroin use is highest amongst lower socioeconomic groups, especially those living in the inner cities. This is believed to be related to the close association between delinquent behavior and illicit drug-seeking activity, combined with the ready availability of such substances in these areas. However, within such environments, high-density areas of organized delinquency, such as street gangs, are frequently associated with decreased drug use. The fact that the overwhelming majority of individuals living in such areas do not become dependent upon mood-altering substances is often ignored, as is the prevalence of heroin use amongst the middle classes in suburbia where obvious delinquent behavior may not be readily apparent.

Simplistic theories pertaining to drug use and race also abound. It is commonly believed that members of minority groups are most likely to be addicted to narcotics, whereas users of other drugs, such as alcohol, cross racial and ethnic barriers. With respect to heroin dependency, Johnson has demonstrated how such beliefs, while appearing to be confirmed upon casual review, cannot be sustained when data are subject to careful scrutiny in the presence of comparable control populations.[3] As described by Johnson, one such study by O'Donnell et al. surveyed approximately 2,500 randomly selected men between the ages of 20 and 30. A review of these data revealed that although blacks are more likely than whites to try heroin, in fact, among current heroin users they were represented less frequently. In this survey, the influence of social class was found to contribute about equally with race in experimentation with heroin, with unemployed whites almost as likely to try heroin as their black counterparts.

The propensity of alcoholism in various ethnic groups has long been studied. Bales, as early as 1944, proposed that at least three crucial factors fostered the development of alcoholism in a particular society: 1) the amount of inner stress and anxiety; 2) the degree to which culture provides alternatives; and 3) the groups' continuing attitudes toward alcohol.[4] Where drinking is 1) clearly differentiated from drunkenness, 2) associated with eating or ritual, 3) divorced from individual efforts to escape personal anxiety or 4) disapproved when accompanied by inappropriate behavior, the incidence of alcoholism is markedly diminished.[5] These concepts have led to explain the relatively high prevalence of alcoholism amongst native Americans and the extremely low levels observed amongst Orientals and those of Jewish extraction.

The acceptance of these stereotypes, however, ignores the obvious. Native Americans are, in fact, quite heterogenous, with many tribes having a much lower prevalence of alcoholism than the nationwide mean. Furthermore, the existence of a definite, and perhaps increasing, prevalence of alcoholism amongst European groups is becoming more frequently recognized. Jones-Saumty et al. in this issue address the attitudes of native American and Caucasian college youths toward problem drinking.[6] Common biases concerning alcoholism are shown in each group's attitudes. While both native Americans and Caucasians attribute problem drinking primarily to the individual although recognizing the importance of external factors, the native American group considered alcoholism as a disease significantly more often than the Caucasian. Native American women considered the development of alcoholism to be more or less "fatalistic."

Are the ethnic and racial differences reported by the ethnographer among populations mainly cultural or do biologic differences exist that can account for such findings? It has long been acknowledged in the laboratory model that strains of mice and rats can be inbred which differ markedly in their preference for or avoidance of alcohol, as well as severity of withdrawal.[7,8] Clinically, Orientals have been found to have higher acetaldehyde levels in their blood than Caucasians. The blushing reaction reported to be more frequent in Orientals after alcohol intake may well be related to increased levels of acetaldehyde serving as a negative reenforcer and making the consumption of alcohol less attractive.[9,10] Significant correlations have also been reported between alcoholism and salivary secretion of ABH blood groups[11] and low platelet monooxidase activity.[12] A causal relationship between these findings and development of alcoholism, however, remains far from confirmed. The existing biologic differences among particular ethnic groups are of interest but cannot be considered at this time to provide sufficient predictive ability to identify those at risk for alcoholism. Broad, sweeping statements concerning drug use amongst these individuals, therefore, become less than helpful.

Since race and social class provide little predictive power in the development of alcoholism or other chemical dependencies, perhaps smaller constellations that cut across these groups, such as family and gender, may allow a better understanding of these conditions. The family has long been considered important in fostering drug use. A consistent profile of those dependent on heroin has been one of impoverished family relationships, marked by early separation of parents, with the maternal influence becoming dominant.[13,14] Alcohol and/or other drug use is often prevalent within the family unit. Hater et al. in this issue of *Advances* review the role of family, religion and personal variables in relationship to long-term outcome after treatment for drug abuse in over 1,000 heroin addicts.[15] With the exception of religion, these investigators found that personal background and family variables were uniquely related to the general well-being of the individual and successful rehabilitation. Greater family resources were consistently associated with favorable outcomes, whereas identification of family problems was negatively correlated.

The families of alcoholics have been found to present a somewhat similar picture as those of heroin users, with higher rates of alcoholism amongst relatives of alcoholics consistently reported. Prior to siding with the nurture side of causality, the biologic factors must also be considered. Studies based on the biologic model of alcoholism have impressibly demonstrated that the role played by the family environment is far from conclusive. The prevalence of alcoholism has been found to be much more frequent in monozygotic than dizygotic twins. The sons of alcoholics separated from their alcoholic parents early in life and raised by foster parents have an almost four-fold risk of becoming alcoholics than adoptees without alcoholic biologic parents. The more severe the father's alcoholism, the greater the possibility for its appearing in the son.[16,17] Recently, the role of heredity in alcoholism has been more clearly defined with the identification of a male-limited trait that tends to be passed only from fathers to sons relatively independent of environment and a "milieu-limited" process that can environmentally influence both the frequency and severity of the alcoholism.[18,19] Clearly, with respect to alcoholism the nature versus nurture controversy cannot be resolved.

If one moves within the family constellation to focus on women, it is surprising, yet true, that only relatively recently has interest developed in studying the characteristics of chemically-dependent women. The tendency to focus on men in both research and treatment efforts is somewhat unusual as surveys of the use of prescribed mood-altering drugs have always found women overrepresented, approximating twice that of men for each psychotropic drug or for any given psychotropic agent.[20,21]

Although profiles of women heroin users have characteristics quite similar to those seen in men, the effects of heroin dependency on women, as well as how they are viewed by society, differ markedly. Since most women dependent upon heroin usually resort to prostitution to support their habit, the damaging effect that this has on the individual's self-esteem, combined with society's condemnation, results in considerable anxiety and estrangement from both family and friends, even when abstinence is obtained.[22] Women alcoholics, while not necessarily needing to engage in prostitution to maintain their alcoholism, suffer, nonetheless, similar emotional trauma and, in fact, show much greater psychopathology and maladjustment than their male counterparts.[23] Covington and Kohen describe the interrelationship between alcohol and sexuality in women.[24] The frequency of sexual dysfunction and sexual abuse demonstrated in the cohort of alcoholic women as compared to controls emphasizes the necessity of a multidimensional approach to the treatment of alcoholism.

Since all of us are part of society, we frequently share, consciously or unconsciously, inherent biases associated with alcoholism and substance abuse. These biases, unfortunately, extend to those caring for the chemically dependent. It is not at all infrequent for counselors working in methadone maintenance programs to have an unconscious bias toward the use of methadone. For this reason, clients on methadone maintenance are prematurely detoxified prior to achieving optimal stability, often with the encouragement of their counselors. Therapeutic communities view methadone maintenance with abhorrence, and abstinence groups treating alcoholics frequently refuse to accept anyone taking a prescribed mood-altering drug despite the improvement in functioning resulting from this treatment. Although the effectiveness of methadone maintenance has resulted in many Alcoholics Anonymous units accepting people on methadone, nonetheless, an unconscious bias is frequently present, resulting in pressure on the individual to detoxify from methadone.

Vannicelli and Hamilton in this issue demonstrate the effect of bias in alcohol-treatment personnel through a role playing workshop using surrogate clients.[25] This technique is much more effective in assessing unconscious bias than the use of questionnaires that allow an individual to easily activate defense mechanisms. The data gathered in this study, which focused on the impact of sexual bias on clinical practice, found women clients to be viewed consistently as having a poorer prognosis than men despite the absence of any differences in the severity of problems. Equally important was the finding that staff perceived problems to be of greater significance when the problem was sex appropriate. Of most interest was the observation that these biases were of greater prevalence in the women counselors. It is not unusual for such beliefs to enter the therapeutic milieu, preventing successful abstinence and rehabilitation.

Finally, although this issue of *Advances* focuses on the social and cultural aspects of substance abuse, it would be inappropriate not to briefly emphasize the interplay between individual psychodynamics and all of the other factors noted above. Although the psychodynamic constructs of the dependencies abound and analytic descriptions of the addictive personality can be easily located, the effectiveness of psychotherapy in managing these dependencies has been far from adequately evaluated. As most of the studies reported in the literature are far from well designed, their findings are difficult to interpret. However, even more recent studies utilizing randomized, controlled techniques reported conflicting findings.[26] With respect to alcoholism, similar confusion exists. Some investigators feel psychotherapy may be harmful as it can deflect attention from the problem of alcoholism, with the client's psychodynamics becoming the focus while the alcoholism continues unabated.[27]

In summary, despite the numerous publications in both the scientific literature and the lay press concerning the ethnographic and the biologic features of addictive behavior, the nature versus nurture controversy is far from resolved. In fact, it never should be for it is really a nonissue. Behavior that leads to the development of dependency on alcohol or other substances is clearly rooted in psychosocial, cultural and biologic realms. Undue attention to any of these areas to the neglect of the others on an individual basis can only lead to a fragmented approach to both prevention and therapy, serving neither the patient nor the therapist. An eclectic approach to the management of chemical dependencies is essential yet all too neglected by those caring for substance abusers. Until these conscious and unconscious biases can be overcome and the complexity of factors leading to an individual's use of alcohol and/or drugs recognized, such controversies will continue and therapy will be far from optimal.

*Barry Stimmel, MD*

## REFERENCES

1. Walters JM. What is Ethnography? In: Atkins C, Beschner G, eds. Ethnography: a research tool for policymakers in the drug and alcohol fields. US Dept Health and Human Services, National Institute on Drug Abuse, Rockville, Maryland, 1980. DHHS Pub. No. (ADM) 80-946, pp. 15-20.
2. Westermeyer J. The role of ethnicity in substance abuse. Advances in Alcohol & Substance Abuse. 1984; 4(1):9-18.
3. Johnson BD. The race, class and irreversibility hypothesis: myths and research about heroin. In: Dunne J, Hayhouse R, eds. The epidemiology of heroin and other narcotics. US Dept Health and Human Services, National Institute on Drug Abuse, Rockville, Maryland, 1977. NIDA Research Monograph No. 16, pp. 51-61.
4. Bales RF. Cultural differences in rates of alcoholism. Q J Studies on Alcohol. 1945; 6:480-99.
5. Zinberg NE. Alcohol addiction: toward a more comprehensive definition. Bean MH, Zinberg NE, eds. In: Dynamic approaches to the understanding and treatment of alcoholism. New York: The Free Press, 1981:97-127.
6. Jones-Saumty DJ, Dru RL, Zeiner AR. Causal attribution of drinking antecedents in American Indian and Caucasian social drinkers. Advances in Alcohol & Substance Abuse. 1984; 4(1):19-28.
7. McClearn GE. The genetic aspects of alcoholism. In: Bourne PG, Fox R, eds. Alcoholism: progress in research and treatment. New York: Academic Press, 1973:337-58.
8. Goldstein DB, Kakihana R. Alcohol withdrawal reactions in mouse strains selectively bred for long or short sleep times. Life Science. 1975; 17:981.
9. Ewing JA, Rouse BA, Pellizzari ED. Alcohol sensitivity and ethnic background. Am J Psychiat. 1974; 131:206-10.
10. Fenna D, Mix L, Schaefer O, Gilbert JA. Ethanol metabolism in various racial groups. Canad Med Assoc J. 1971; 105:472-76.
11. Camps FE, Doff BE, Lincoln PJ. Frequencies of secretors and non-secretors of ABH group substances among 1,000 alcoholic patients. Brit Med J. 1969; 4:457-59.
12. Major LF, Murphy DL. Platelet and plasma amine oxidase activity in alcoholic individuals. Brit J Psychiat. 1978; 132:548-54.
13. Chien I, Gerard DL, Lee RS et al. The road to H: narcotics, delinquency & social policy. New York: Basic Books, 1964.
14. Vaillant GE. Parent-child cultural disparity and drug addiction. J Nerv Ment Dis. 1968; 142:534-39.
15. Hater JJ, Singh BK, Simpson DD. Influence of family and religion on long-term outcomes among opioid addicts. Advances in Alcohol & Substance Abuse. 1984; 4(1):29-40.
16. Cadoret RJ, Cain CA, Grove W. Development of alcoholism in adoptees raised apart from biologic parents. Arch Gen Psychiat. 1980; 37:561-63.
17. Goodwin DW. Is alcoholism hereditary? New York: Oxford University Press, 1976.
18. Cloninger CR, Bohman M, Sigvardsson S. Inheritance of alcohol abuse: cross-fostering analysis of adopted men. Arch Gen Psychiat. 1981; 38:861-68.
19. Bohman M, Sigvardsson S, Cloninger CR. Maternal inheritance of alcohol abuse: cross-fostering analysis of adopted women. Arch Gen Psychiat. 1981; 38:965-69.
20. Parry H. The use of psychotropic drugs by U.S. adults. Public Health Service Reports. 1968; 83:799-810.

21. Parry HJ, Balter MB, Mellinger GD, Cisen IH et al. National patterns of psychotherapeutic drug use. Arch Gen Psych. 1973; 28:769-83.

22. Maglin A. Sex role differences in heroin addiction. Social Casework. 1974; 55:160-67.

23. Beckman LJ. The psychosocial characteristics of alcoholic women. Drug Abuse Alcohol Review. 1978; 1:1-11.

24. Covington SS, Kohen J. Women, alcohol, and sexuality. Advances in Alcohol & Substance Abuse. 1984; 4(1):41-56.

25. Vannicelli M, Hamilton G. Sex-role values and bias in alcohol treatment personnel. Advances in Alcohol & Substance Abuse. 1984; 4(1):57-68.

26. Psychotherapy for methadone maintained opiate addicts: A report of two studies. National Institute on Drug Abuse, US Dept Health and Human Services. Alcohol, Drug Abuse and Mental Health Administration, Rockville, Maryland. DHHS Pub. No. (ADM) 83-1289, p. 23.

27. Vaillant GE. Dangers of psychotherapy in the treatment of alcoholism. In: Dynamic approaches to the understanding and treatment of alcoholism. Op. Cit., pp. 36-54.

# The Role of Ethnicity
# in Substance Abuse

Joseph Westermeyer, MD, PhD

**ABSTRACT.** Ethnicity can be a confusing concept. In part, it includes inherited characteristics such as race. Certain other aspects are learned, such as religion, language, attitudes, values, or customs. National origin of oneself or one's kin can be a component of ethnicity. Group affiliation and participation in certain ritual and ceremony are also involved in ethnicity. Substance abuse and dependence may undermine certain aspects of ethnicity and ethnic affiliations, by interfering with traditional values, attitudes, preferred behaviors, and interpersonal relationships. Substance abuse leads to the evolution of new values, attitudes and behaviors. These are remarkably similar (though not identical) from one chemically dependent person to another. In some cases the chemically dependent person remains a social isolate, while in other cases the individual joins with others to create a subculture in which the drug or alcohol centered values, attitudes and behaviors are shared.

Treatment for alcoholism or drug abuse—if successful—produces crisis in ethnic identity for many people. Drug centered values and behaviors are directly confronted in the treatment process, and affiliation with alcohol or drug subcultures is specifically undermined. This may create a state of anomie—with its attendant confusion, anxiety, and loss. Out of this turmoil some individuals resume their original, childhood ethnic identities and affiliations (though often more accentuated than before). Others assume new ethnic identities or affiliations.

## DEFINING A COMMON GROUND

*Ethnicity.* This term refers to a group's attitudes, values, and preferred behaviors—especially as these are distinct from the preferences of others. It sometimes infers the added commonality of

Joseph Westermeyer is a Professor in the Department of Psychiatry, University of Minnesota, Minneapolis, Minnesota 55455.

This study was supported in part by the National Institutes of Alcohol Abuse and Alcoholism (grant number 1 R01 AA 0934-01), the Minnesota Medical Foundation, and the National Institutes of Drug Abuse (grant number 5 T01 DA 00023-02).

9

language, religion, race, and national origin, especially in static populations in which there exists little cross-ethnic marriage, adoption, or contact through work, education, residence, shared interests, or friendship.

It requires an understanding attitude, rapport, and time to obtain information regarding a patient's current or past ethnicity. Especially in a multi-ethnic urban society, there are so many blends of ethnicity that simplistic categorization of a given individual is often not possible. In multi-ethnic societies it is common to encounter context-specific ethnic behavior. For example, many people behave as "majority members" or "mainstream Americans" at the workplace, while maintaining their own preferred values or behaviors at home, on vacation, or during holidays. Elsewhere I have referred to the example of an American Indian man who abstained from alcohol in his middle-class neighborhood, did "White drinking" with his fellow construction workers, and engaged in "Indian drinking" when visiting his relatives on the reservation during vacations.[1]

*Nationality.* This may refer to the nation in which a person is born, or to the nation in which one's ancestors were born. Nationality may reveal only limited information regarding a person's values and attitudes. The concept of "nation" in recent times refers more to geography than ethnicity. For example, there are scores of ethnic groups within all the nation-states of the world. As technology spreads and standards of living increase, certain national characteristics are reinforced through national school systems, the mass media, communication and transportation systems, one or a few national languages, and a shared political system. This development may blur differences within countries while accentuating differences among countries—even adjacent countries with similar political orientations. Like race, nationality is not amenable to change.

*Religion.* Religion is a valuable ethnic concept in the clinical setting since it refers to group affiliation and values. This is especially true with people who were enculturated within a certain religion and are currently practicing it. Many substance abusers are not currently practicing a religion, typically having abandoned a religion which was previously practiced.[2,3]

*Language.* Linguistic preference may give some indication of group affiliation. However, it can cut across racial, ethnic, national, and religious boundaries. For example, the assignment of people as "Spanish speaking" or "Spanish surname" can refer to the following: people from North America, Central America, South America,

Europe, and Asia; people who are racially Caucasian, Negroid, American Indian, Asian, or a mixture of these; and people who ascribe to such widely variable religions as animism, Judaism, Catholicism, and Protestantism. It can even apply to people whose Spanish-speaking ancestors migrated to the United States generations ago, and who themselves no longer speak Spanish.

*Race.* Technically, race involves genetic differences among subspecies. In the clinical context race usually refers primarily to skin color and physiognomy, however. Racial characteristics do not provide any direct information regarding an individual's values, behavior, or preferred modes of interpersonal relationships. Especially in a multi-ethnic urban setting, physiognomy can be more misleading than enlightening since education and social mobility may erode sociocultural differences among racial groups. Increased cross-racial adoption of children and cross-racial marriage have further complicated the issue. The folk terms "Oreo-cookie" (i.e., racial Black with Euroamerican cultural affiliations) or "apple" (i.e, racial American Indian with Euroamerican cultural identity) indicate the potential discontinuity between race and ethnicity.

Despite the apparent simplicity of racial categorizations, even these are not readily determined. For example, racial determinations made by the admission clerks at University of Minnesota Hospitals were assessed for 63 American Indian People, all of whom were one-half to full blooded Indian. They viewed themselves as ethnic Chippewa or Sioux. The clerks marked the racial category "Indian" in 16 cases and the racial group "White" in 9 cases; they did not make any racial entry in 38 cases.

*Minority Groups.* There is no clear consensus regarding what comprises a minority group. Valien has suggested that the term minority group is used when individual distinctions are being made, while the term ethnic groups is used when the distinctions are not invidious.[4] Wirth has further remarked, "Minority status carries with it the exclusion from full participation in the life of the society."[5] Literature on the subject indicates that the concept minority consists of a variety of characteristics including ethnicity, race, national origin, religion and language.[6-11]

From a strictly statistical vantage point, all Americans belong to a minority group of one kind or another by virtue of gender, age, religion, occupation, *et cetera*. Current use of the term, however, conveys a sense of political struggle, or gaining access to scarce resources within the majority society, or solving social problems and meeting social needs that are not being met by the society at large. From this vantage point, the elderly may be seen as a minority, though they come from many ethnic origins. Even women, who comprise a numerical majority in our society, may in a sense be a minority group when their special needs are being ignored, as may occur with alcoholic women. By the same token, groups that are clearly in a numerical minority—such as Caucasian Episcopalian people of English origin—may not currently consider themselves a minority, since there is currently no political, social or financial need to do so.

*Culture.* This concept involves a variety of social-behavior elements, ranging from a group's technology to their religion and philosophy. Cultural elements are learned, rather than inherited. Symbolically they are strongly valued and are passed on from one generation to the next. One classification of cultural elements is as follows:

- technology: transportation, housing, food supply, tools, food, and clothes;
- social institutions: family, clan, village/band/neighborhood, friendship, marriage, education, guilds, industry, political organization.
- communication: language, clothing styles, grooming, nonverbal behavior, conformity/deviance;
- psychosocial: world view, beliefs, values, attitudes, ideal norms; actual normals, role, status, prestige, ritual, ceremony, symbols, holidays, recreation, play, "time out."

## EFFECT OF ALCOHOLISM
## AND DRUG ABUSE ON ETHNICITY

*Ethnicity-of-Origin.* Certain values and attitudes are universal among all ethnic groups. These include responsibility to the family and the group, care of children and the sick and disabled, respect for others and their personal belongings, participation in social and/or religious rituals, assignment of social roles, and ideal cultural norms which may not always coincide with behavioral norms. Other values and attitudes differ widely among ethnic groups, such as the viewpoint towards outsiders.

The demands of alcoholism or drug abuse conflict with ethnic values and attitudes in various ways. The individual gradually places a higher and higher value on the chemical experience. The latter rises in the person's hierarchy of priorities. It may displace core values that have been important to the person, such as punctuality or neatness or truthfulness. The individual typically spends more time in obtaining resources to purchase the drug, more time using the drug, and more time in an intoxicated state, while spending less time in social or religious ritual, less resources on the family or group, and less involvement in the service of others. Of course, the extent and rate at which this exchange takes place varies from person to person.

*Substance Abuse Subcultures.* Chemically dependent people come to share a group of values, attitudes, and behaviors that are rather remarkable in their similarity.[11-17] Individual differences begin to blur as they spend increasingly larger proportions of their life seeking, using, and intoxicated on chemicals. Their relationships with others become marked by much manipulation and hostile dependency. This occurs despite the nature of their previous interpersonal relationships, and subsequent interpersonal relationships if they can persist in abstinence, which are as varied as their many individual personalities and ethnic groups.

As a consequence of these behavioral and personality changes, drug and alcohol dependent people become progressively estranged from their friends and family. Some individuals do not seek out the affiliation of other chemically dependent people (for example, many housewives and professional persons). Other chemically dependent persons attach themselves to a group whose members share their values, attitudes, and preferred behaviors.

Substance abuse subcultures resemble other groups in society. They accept and initiate new members into their ranks. Affiliation with the group may involve in-group characteristics such as special words, dress, greetings, attitudes or behaviors. Reciprocity and exchange take place, such as information regarding jobs or other sources of money, access to inexpensive but potent alcohol or drugs, and sometimes sharing of the alcohol or drugs.

These alcohol or drug groups tend to be more fragile than family, kin, neighborhood, or work groups. Once a member proves a liability to the group or cannot contribute to the group, affiliation and loyalty rapidly disappear. Weaker members may be parasitized by the needy strong.

Within some substance abuse groups, there is more inter-racial and inter-ethnic admixture than in the society at large. For example, Skid Row areas are usually inhabited by all racial and ethnic groups. A similar observation has been made in Asian opium dens where various ethnic groups were found to socialize together although similar ethnic contacts elsewhere in the society were infrequent and highly formalized.[17] Sexual mating across ethnic boundaries may occur more often in such subcultures than is usual elsewhere in society.

Previous ethnic values, attitudes, and behaviors are not totally forgotten nor irrevocably abandoned during this time. For example one addicted Chicano man stated that for him being a Chicano (with his obligations to family, neighborhood and church) was "put on the shelf" for the time being, adding that "I might go back to it sometime in the future." A Navaho woman completely abandoned contact with her reservation, ceased attending pow-wows, and spent most of her time with narcotic addicts from other ethnic backgrounds; however, she refused to sell certain Navaho jewelry that had been passed down to her within the family, even when she was most in need of money to make a narcotic drug purchase in order to stave off a withdrawal period. An Irish-American alcoholic man abandoned contacts with his family, church, and neighborhood, but continued to wear a holy medal around his neck and carried rosary beads in his pocket.

## *ROLE OF ETHNICITY IN REHABILITATION*

*Post-Treatment Anomie.* Religious or ethnic affiliation is sometimes seen merely as another form of dependency. To paraphrase this view: if religio-mania replaces dipsomania, the basic underlying psychopathology remains the same. This suggests that true maturity evolves only when all dependencies have been abandoned, to be replaced by a condition of secure independence.

Another viewpoint suggests that these psychologically oriented theories are overly simplistic and ignore complex social issues. As the addicted individual attempts to maintain abstinence, chemical dependency related behaviors must be abandoned. These behaviors cannot change unless chemical dependency related values and attitudes also change. Deprived of these familiar values, attitudes, and behaviors, the individual becomes enmeshed in a condition known as anomie. This is a state of both psychological and social disorientation with lack of references to what is right or wrong, valuable or worthless, desirable or undesirable. The individual struggling to maintain abstinence is faced with new social situations in which norms related to substance abuse no longer apply. Depression often ensues, and sometimes even anomic suicide.[18] MacIver has said of anomie that it "signifies the state of mind of one who has been pulled up from his moral roots, who has no longer any standards but only disconnected urges, who has no longer any sense of continuity, of folk, of obligation."[19] This suggests that substance abuse is not resolved merely by psychological resolution of dependency strivings, but by the evolution of values, attitudes, and behavior not related to the substance abuse life style.

*Reversion to Prior Ethnicity.* Most recovering alcoholics and drug addicts resume abandoned values, attitudes, and behaviors from their past. Sometimes this takes place with greater enthusiasm than had been present before becoming chemically dependent. For example, many Irish-American alcoholics begin an active role in church, family, and neighborhood activities. Recovering Chippewa alcoholics spend time with other recovering Chippewa alcoholics, do bead work, teach the Chippewa language, attend pow-wows, join a drum group, or become active in Indian associations. Recovering rural Asian opium addicts begin again attending ceremonies related to birth, marriage, and death, resume long abandoned economic activities, and again participate in village political decisions.

*Need for a New Ethnicity.* Some individuals became chemically dependent at such an early age that they were never fully enculturated into their own ethnic group. Others were raised within families that did not provide an enculturation learning experience. And still other recovering people have such negative feelings about the values and attitudes and behaviors of their own ethnic group that they do not wish to resume affiliation with the group whence they came. Such individuals may seek a new identity. This often takes the guise of a religious conversion to a new faith, which in turn may lead to new friendships and behaviors.

## ETHNIC ASPECTS OF TREATMENT

Minority alcoholics and drug abusers frequently do not seek help in majority treatment facilities.[20-22] In those instances where they do, however, there have not been any demonstrated instances of biased treatment.[23-25] Thus, the majority stance has often been "Take it or leave it: we are here for people of all backgrounds, and if they do not utilize our resources it is not our responsibility."

There are alternatives, however. One has been to establish minority-run and staffed treatment programs. These have been successful.[26] Of course, this approach requires a sufficiently large population to justify a separate program. Almost by definition, minority people often comprise small communities which do not justify separate services.

Another alternative has been to hire a number of minority people in the program. This has been described for medical programs,[27] but has also involved substance abuse programs. Ordinarily there is no patient assignment solely by race. Nevertheless, minority people attend such programs in larger numbers and at earlier, more treatable stages. Perhaps the coworker status among majority and minority staff helps majority staff become more sensitive and helpful to minority patients.

Occasionally most treatment programs encounter patients from unfamiliar ethnic backgrounds. The therapeutic process may nonetheless proceed well if the ethnic difference is not too great, or if there is a common language, education, or other cultural bonds between staff and patient. In some cases referral to another, more appropriate program will serve best the patient.

## CONCLUSION

1. Ethnicity is a concept which cuts across many other related concepts, including race, culture, language, family affiliation and social characteristics. It involves values, social identity, morality and preference.
2. Substance abuse is usually seen as producing biological, psychological, and sometimes social impairment. However, ethnic reverberations are not usually appreciated. Some substance abusers accommodate to their loss of ethnicity by joining a subcultural group of substance abusers. Others merely become isolated and alienated from their ethnic group.
3. Recovery from substance abuse usually involves certain crises which can be appreciated from an ethnic perspective. One of these is anomie: the loss of deep seated, highly valued notions about the world, the purpose of living, and good ends to be achieved.

4. Most recovering substance abusers return to their prior ethnicity, perhaps with some modifications, but often with renewed or even novel intensity. A few adopt a new ethnic identity.

5. Substance abusers are more apt to be attracted into a treatment facility which has ethnic peers on its staff (i.e., people whom they trust, to whom they can relate, with whom they can communicate and identify).

6. Ethnic programs do not appear to have any better treatment outcomes than do majority or "non-ethnic"* programs. However, they do attract more ethnic minority people into treatment and thus do help more minority peoples.

## REFERENCES

1. Westermeyer J. Options regarding alcohol use among the Chippewa Amer. J. Orthopsychiatry. 1975; 42:398-403.

2. Schlingensiepen W, Kasl SU. Helpseeking behavior of male college students with emotional problems. Soc. Psychiatry. 1970; 1:25-34.

3. Westermeyer J, Walzer V. Drug usage: An alternative to religion? Dis. Nervous System. 1975; 36:492-5.

4. Valien P. Minority, minority group. In: Gould J and Kolb WL, eds. A dictionary of the social sciences. New York: Free Press, 1967:432-3.

5. Wirth L. The problem of minority groups. In: Linton R, ed. The Science of Man in the World Crisis. New York: Columbia Univ. Press, 1945:347.

6. Schermerhorn RA. These Our People. Boston: Health, 1949.

7. Allende MF. Non-ethnics. J. Amer. Med. Assoc. 1973; 223:440.

8. Igartua RJ. Ethnic identification. Annals Internal Medicine. 1973; 78:614.

9. Reed TE. Ethnic classification of Mexican Americans Science. 1974; 185:283.

10. Ferris M. Desegregating health statistics. Amer. J. Public Health 1973; 63:477-89.

11. Chase HC. Desegregating health statistics. Amer. J. Public Health 1973; 63:836-37.

12. Hertz E, Hutheesing O. At the edge of society: The nominal culture of urban hotel isolates. Urban Anthropology. 1975; 14:317-32.

13. Kuttner R, Lorincz A. Alcoholism and addiction in urbanized Sioux Indians. Mental Hygiene. 1967; 51:530-42.

14. Westermeyer J. Chippewa and majority alcoholism in the Twin Cities: A comparison. J. Nervous Mental Dis. 1972; 155:322-72.

15. Dumont MP. Tavern culture: The sustenance of homeless men. Amer. J. Orthopsychiatry. 1967; 37:938-45.

16. Finestone H. Cats, kicks, and color. Social Problems. 1957; 5:3-13.

17. Westermeyer J. Opium dens: A social resource for addicts in Laos. Arch. Gen. Psychiat. 1974; 31:237-40.

18. Durkheim E. Suicide. London: Routledge and Kegan Paul, 1952.

19. MacIver RM. The ramparts we guard. New York: Macmillan Press, 1950.

20. Vitals MM. Culture patterns of drinking in Negro and White alcoholics. Dis. Nervous System. 1968; 29:391-2.

---

*Of course, no programs are "non-ethnic." Even majority programs reflect the predominant ethnic influences of the area, whether that be Texan WASP, Minnesota Lutheran Scandinavian, or Louisiana Catholic French.

21. Lowe GD, Hodges HE. Race and the treatment of alcoholism in a southern state. Social Problems. 1972; 20:240-52.
22. Westermeyer J. Use of a social indicator system to assess alcoholism among Indian people in Minnesota. Amer. J. Drug Alcohol Abuse. 1976; 3:447-56.
23. Lowe GD, Alston JP. An analysis of racial differences in services to alcoholics in a southern clinic. Hosp. Community Psychiatry. 1973; 24:547-51.
24. Chegwidden M, Flaherty BJ. Aboriginal versus non-Aboriginal alcoholics in an alcohol withdrawal unit. Med. J. Austr. 1977; 1:699-703.
25. Hoffman H, Noem AA. Adjustment of Chippewa Indian alcoholics to a predominantly White treatment program. Psychol. Rep. 1975; 37:1284-86.
26. Shore J, Kinzie JD, Hampson JL, et al. Psychiatric epidemiology in an Indian village. Psychitry. 1973; 36:70-81.
27. Westermeyer J, Tanner R, Smelker J. Change in health care services of Indian Americans. Minnesota Medicine. 1974; 57:732-34.

# Causal Attribution of Drinking Antecedents in American Indian and Caucasian Social Drinkers

Deborah J. Jones-Saumty, MS
Ralph L. Dru, MD
Arthur R. Zeiner, PhD

**ABSTRACT.** Sixty-five American Indian and 100 Caucasian college students were tested with Beckman's rating scale for antecedents of drinking.[1] Subjects were social drinkers who had had no previous alcohol-related problems (arrests, accidents, etc.). They were matched on age, education, and drinking history. The scale addresses beliefs about drinking and its related causes—internal and external. Results indicate only one major difference between Indians and Caucasians (alcoholism as an illness was rated higher by Indians), while similarities in rating patterns were found in comparing our college sample to college students from the Los Angeles area tested by Beckman. American Indian college students were significantly different in their casual attribution of drinking problems from white college students in Los Angeles.

The authors are affiliated with the Department of Psychiatry and Behavioral Sciences, University of Oklahoma Health Sciences Center, Oklahoma City, Oklahoma. Reprint requests should be addressed to: Arthur R. Zeiner, PhD, MS, Department of Psychiatry and Behavioral Sciences, University of Oklahoma Health Sciences Center, OMH Research Building, 306R, P. O. Box 26901, Oklahoma City, OK 73190.

Some of these data were presented at the 20th International Congress on Applied Psychology, Edinburgh, Scotland, July, 1982.

We gratefully acknowledge the cooperation and assistance of Linda Beckman, PhD and her laboratory staff in supplying additional data and literature for our study. We also thank Dr. Larry Hochhaus, Department of Psychology, Oklahoma State University, for his supervision and comments during data collection and preparation of this manuscript.

## INTRODUCTION

Research on attribution theory has focused on the perceived causes of other persons' behavior. Thibaut and Riecken, in a classic paper, suggested that causal attributions play a central role in human behavior.[2] Attribution research grew out of convergence of many diverse areas, coupled with a growing awareness of a common core of problems. Some of these areas included Heider's early writings on naive psychology,[3] Rotter's research on locus of control[4] and Bem's work on self-perception.[5] According to Kelly,[6] ascribing causal attribution amounts to a particular causal explanation of effects such as reactions or responses, judgments, and evaluations. Predominantly, attribution research has dealt with problems in social psychology. However, some recent studies have looked at the relationship between locus of control and causal attributions of personal behavior. Taylor and Koivumaki[7] found that attributions about personal positive behaviors were more internally oriented whereas attributions about personal negative behaviors were more externally oriented. Similarly, Weiner and his colleagues[8] have suggested that internal attributions, relative to external, heighten effective reactions such as pride for success and shame for failure. Replicative studies have been inconclusive.[9,10,11]

There is a paucity of information about how persons in the general population perceive alcoholism and/or alcohol-related problems. Much of the social stigma associated with alcoholism can be explained by the fact that nonalcoholics generally attribute the cause of the disease internally to alcoholics.[1] In general, Beckman[1] found that nonalcoholic women assigned major responsibility for problem drinking internally to the person doing the drinking. However, several causes were rated as important factors responsible for problem drinking. Female college students, who were social drinkers, were more likely to perceive alcohol-related problems due to external factors than were middle-aged female social drinkers. Additional studies have examined causal attributions for drinking in both alcoholics and nonalcoholics.[12,13,14] Results with alcoholics have been inconsistent. Clinical evidence suggests that alcoholics deny personal responsibility for their drinking and therefore assign causation to external factors. Conversely, cognitive-behavioral therapists argue that alcoholics tend to view themselves negatively and thus, take the blame for their own drinking problem without giving much consideration to external influences.[14]

American Indians, as a group, have a higher proportion of alcohol problems than the general population.[15,16,17] Studies on American Indians and the component factors of alcohol abuse are extremely sparse. Cultural characteristics such as retention of traditional ceremonies, rituals, and beliefs (resulting in acculturation difficulties), and a familial history of alcoholism have been suggested as possible causal factors for the Indian alcohol abuse problem.[18,19,20] There are a number of causal factors (physiological, psychological and/or sociocultural) which may account for Indian alcohol problems. Past research has concentrated almost exclusively on Indian alcoholics. Therefore, many of the conclusions drawn from such studies are merely post hoc observations. By studying Indian social drinkers and their causal attributions for problem drinking, we may be able to delineate some precipitating factors in Indian alcohol abuse.

The aims of this study were to investigate beliefs about the causes of problem drinking in social drinker college students by (a) attempting to replicate the pattern of causal attribution found by Beckman in her original study, and (b) extending the investigation by adding a group of American Indian college student social drinkers. Due to cultural differences (traditional background, views of drinking, and varied drinking styles), we expected differences in the causal attribution of alcohol problems between Indian and Caucasian subjects.

## METHOD

*Subjects.* Sixty-five American Indian and 100 Caucasian college student social drinkers were tested with a rating scale for antecedents of problem drinking developed by Beckman.[1] Both groups consisted of approximately 40% males and 60% females. Subjects were recruited from undergraduate students at three Oklahoma colleges as part of a large-scale study assessing the psychological and drinking behavior profiles of Indians and Caucasians. They were matched on age, years of education, and level of alcohol consumption. The mean age of the Indian group was 19.53 ± 4.26 years, and their average years of education were 13.15 ± 1.30. Caucasian subjects had a mean age of 19.65 ± 2.68 years, while they had 13.51 ± 1.22 average years of education. The average amount of absolute alcohol consumed per drinking episode was 0.67 ± 1.32 ozs. for the Indian group and 0.66 ± 1.14 ozs. for the Caucasian group. All subjects were volunteers and considered themselves to be social drinkers (no previous alcohol-related problems such as arrests, accidents, hospitalization, or treatment for alcohol abuse). According to the Cahalan classification system,[22] all subjects were social drinkers at either the heavy, moderate, or light level. Indian subjects identified themselves as at least one-half Indian blood of any tribe native to North America. Caucasians were those subjects who identified themselves as such, and were not of Hispanic, Negro, Asian, or Indian descent.

Additionally, two groups (N = 38 each) composed of college-age female social drinkers, matched on age and education, were compared to Beckman's sample of 58 normal drinking college females. The mean age and years of education was 19.63 ± 1.39 and 13.03 ± 1.22 for the Indian group and 19.87 ± 3.49 and 13.55 ± 1.35 for the Caucasian group. Beckman's sample of college-age social drinker females had a mean age of 21.16 years, with a range of 18 to 29 years.

*Procedure.* After completing an informed consent form, a battery of psychological and drinking questionnaires were administered in group settings of no more than 20 subjects. The questions relevant to this paper involved personal beliefs about responsibility for alcoholism, and they were included as part of an alcohol consumption and drinking behavior survey. Subjects were asked to rate the importance of seven causal factors relative to alcoholism in the general population: (a) Other People, (b) Distressing Event, (c) Environment, (d) Heredity, (e) Self, (f) Illness/Disease, and (g) Fate. Ratings were made on a 4-point scale ranging from unimportant (1) to very important (4). The scale was developed by Beckman[1] after a thorough examination of various alcoholism theories and the literature on attribution theory.

## RESULTS

The data from the seven causal factors on Indian and Caucasian social drinkers were subjected to analysis of variance. The overall F ratio was not significant (p = .25). Independent group t-tests were performed to determine significant differences between mean antecedent ratings. Z-tests were done comparing our experimental groups with Beckman's group of normal drinking college females.

Causal attributions for problem drinking were strikingly similar across ethnic groups. Indians and Caucasians were found to differ significantly on only one causal factor. The Indian group rated alcoholism as an illness/disease significantly higher (t = 3.01, p < .01) than did the Caucasian group. Both groups attributed problem drinking to the person himself, while also rating fate as the least important factor for alcoholism in the general population.

The antecedent rating scale used in this study was devised by Beckman and her colleagues at UCLA. She tested a group of normal social drinking college females on the antecedent scale. The attribution pattern of Beckman's sample placed primary importance on self as a causal factor in alcoholism, while placing fate as a very unimportant causal factor. Our Caucasian group replicated this pattern of attribution on seven factors. However, the Indian group maintained attributions consistent with those of the Beckman group on the most important and unimportant factors, while rating the middle factors quite differently.

There were significant mean differences on four of the seven causal factors in comparisons between the Beckman sample and our Caucasian group. Caucasian social drinker college students from Oklahoma rated heredity (z = 2.91, p < .002), self (z = 2.48, p < .005), illness/disease (z = 7.76, p < .0000005) and fate (z = 2.24, p < .015) as being more important in causing problem drinking than did students from the Los Angeles area. There was only one significant difference on mean antecedent ratings between Indian social drinker college students and Beckman's sample of Los Angeles college students. The Indian group rated alcoholism as being an illness or disease significantly more often than did the Los Angeles sample (z = 3.48, p < .0005). Table 1 displays the mean antecedent ratings for our Indian and Caucasian groups, and Beckman's group of normal drinking college students.

In keeping with our aim to replicate Beckman's 1979 study, we collected data on two groups (N = 38 each) of female social drinker college students (Indian and Caucasian). Analysis of variance revealed an overall F ratio of 0.91 which was nonsignificant. Analysis by t-test showed only one significant difference between our Indian and Caucasian groups. American Indian females rated fate as being an important causal factor in problem drinking significantly more often than did Caucasian females (t = 2.45, p < .01).

By comparing our two female experimental groups with Beckman's female sample, we found only one significant difference be-

## TABLE 1

### ANTECEDENT RATING PATTERNS FOR THREE GROUPS OF SOCIAL DRINKER COLLEGE STUDENTS

| | Beckman (1979) Normal College Females (N=58) | Jones-Saumty et al. (1984) Caucasian Social Drinkers (N=100) | Jones-Saumty et al. (1984) Indian Social Drinkers (N=65) |
|---|---|---|---|
| A. Self | $3.36 \pm 0.72$ | $3.71 \pm 0.52$ | $3.63 \pm 0.68$ |
| B. Distressing Event | $3.07 \pm 0.62$ | $3.16 \pm 0.80$ | $3.09 \pm 0.99$ |
| C. Environment | $3.00 \pm 0.79$ | $2.96 \pm 0.89$ | $3.03 \pm 1.03$ |
| D. Other People | $2.64 \pm 0.79$ | $2.68 \pm 0.92$ | $2.95 \pm 0.98$ |
| E. Illness | $1.39 \pm 0.65$ | $2.50 \pm 1.15$ | $2.85 \pm 0.73$ |
| F. Heredity | $1.33 \pm 0.66$ | $1.78 \pm 1.28$ | $2.11 \pm 1.54$ |
| G. Fate | $1.07 \pm 0.32$ | $1.34 \pm 1.13$ | $1.40 \pm 0.81$ |

tween our Caucasian females and the Beckman sample. Our white female group rated alcoholism as an illness/disease significantly more than did white females from the Los Angeles area ($z = 2.23$, $p < .015$). Similarly, the Indian female group rated alcoholism as an illness significantly more often than did white females in Beckman's sample ($z = 3.00$, $p < .002$). These results are depicted in Table 2.

## DISCUSSION

Both Indian and Caucasian college-age social drinkers attributed problem drinking primarily to the individual, while also viewing external factors (distressing events, environment, etc.) as concomitant influences on problem drinking. These findings replicate those of Beckman.[1] However, consistent with our hypothesis, the Indian group did show a different pattern of attribution ratings for problem drinking relative to both their matched Caucasian counterparts from Oklahoma and the social drinker sample in Beckman's study. Our results indicate a tendency on the part of nonalcoholics to attribute problem drinking in the general population to the individual doing the drinking. Additionally, the general tendency of social drinkers was to discount the influence of fate on problem drinking. Another similarity to Beckman's study was that our sample also rated several causes as being possibly responsible for problem drinking in the general population. These findings are consistent with Kelley's assertion that an extremely negative effect, such as alcoholism, generally evokes a multiple causal schema.[6]

American Indian social drinkers rated alcoholism as an illness/disease significantly more often than did Caucasian social drinkers. This would seem to indicate a tendency to view alcoholism as an environmentally-induced (external) disease. Consistent with these findings, Indians have been found to have a stronger orientation toward chance control than Caucasians.[21] While Indians attribute primary responsibility for alcoholism to the drinker himself, it is clear that alcohol abuse still occupies a position as an "unknown quantity" among contemporary Indian social drinkers. Thus, Indians often accept the societal explanations for lack of something better. Unfortunately, many tribes today still have no established codes governing alcohol consumption among their members (with the notable exception of the government-imposed prohibition on federal reservations). This lack of tribal regulations may partially

TABLE 2

MEAN ANTECEDENT RATINGS FOR THREE GROUPS OF
FEMALE COLLEGE STUDENT SOCIAL DRINKERS

| | Jones-Saumty & Zeiner, 1984 | | Beckman, 1979 |
| | Indians | Caucasians | College Females |
| | (N=38) | (N=38) | (N=58) |
|---|---|---|---|
| A. Other People | 2.79 ± 0.76 | 2.37 ± 1.75 | 2.64 ± 0.79 |
| B. Distressing Event | 3.05 ± 1.00 | 3.24 ± 1.00 | 3.07 ± 0.62 |
| C. Environment | 2.74 ± 0.96 | 2.95 ± 0.76 | 3.00 ± 0.79 |
| D. Heredity | 1.97 ± 0.99 | 1.92 ± 0.96 | 1.33 ± 0.66 |
| E. Self | 3.55 ± 0.78 | 3.63 ± 3.67 | 3.36 ± 0.72 |
| F. Illness | 2.89 ± 1.08 | 2.55 ± 1.14 | 1.39 ± 0.65 |
| G. Fate | 1.37 ± 0.67 | 1.08 ± 0.28 | 1.07 ± 0.32 |

explain the varied attributional rating pattern of the Indian group. While the most and least important causal factors were the same for both Indians and Caucasians, the remaining factors were rated consistently across both groups of Caucasian social drinkers (Oklahoma and California) but differently within the Indian group. Thus, Indians seem to adhere to societal explanations for alcohol abuse to a certain extent, while still exhibiting some confusion over alternative explanations for alcoholism and alcohol abuse.

In keeping with our replication of Beckman's work,[1] we compared two groups of female social drinkers from both our samples with a group of female normal drinkers in the Beckman study. The pattern of attribution was similar across groups with the exception of the environment and illness/disease factors. Beckman's group of female drinkers rated environment as the third most important causal factor in problem drinking as did Oklahoma Caucasian students, while the Indian sample rated environment fifth of seven causal factors. Interestingly, the Indian females viewed fate as an important causal factor more often than Caucasian females. Perhaps the regional differences between urban Los Angeles and suburban/rural Oklahoma may partially account for these attributional differences. However, these results also provide additional evidence for Kelley's multiple causal schema.[6] While primary responsibility may be attributed to the individual doing the drinking, external/environmental factors may also be seen as having significant importance. This would seem to be especially true for Indian females.

In summary, results of this study replicate those of Beckman's,[1] with our social drinker sample showing stronger causal attribution ratings in many instances. Both American Indian and Caucasian social drinkers attributed problem drinking primarily to the individual while also attributing important causal influence to external factors. Cross-culturally, only one significant difference in causal attribution emerged. The Indian group rated alcoholism as an illness/disease significantly more often than did Caucasians. Attribution rating patterns were similar for Caucasian social drinkers (Oklahoma) and Beckman's normal drinker group, while American Indian rating patterns were very dissimilar to both groups. Female social drinkers consistently rated internal causation high, while American Indian females also believed strongly in the effects of fate on causing problem drinking. These findings lend support to Kelly's assertion[6] of a multiple causal schema for explaining negative behaviors such as alcoholism.

## REFERENCES

1. Beckman LJ. Beliefs about the causes of alcohol-related problems among alcoholic and nonalcoholic women. *J Clin Psychology* 1979;93:663-670.

2. Thibaut JW, Riecken HW. Some determinants and consequences of the perception of social causality. *J Personality* 1955;24:113-133.

3. Heider F. The psychology of interpersonal relations. New York: Wiley, 1958.

4. Rotter JB. Generalized expectancies for internal versus external control of reinforcement. *Psychological Monographs* 1966;80-1-28.

5. Bem DJ. Self-perception theory. *Advances in Experimental Social Psychology* 1972;6:1-62.

6. Kelley HH. The process of causal attribution. *American Psychologist* 1973; Feb.:107-128.

7. Taylor SE, Kivumaki JH. The perception of self and others: Acquaintanceship, affect and actor-observer differences. *J Per Soc Psychology* 1976;33:403-408.

8. Weiner B, Nierenberg R, Goldstein M. Social learning (locus of control) versus attributional (causal stability) interpretations of expectancy of success. *J Personality* 1976; 44:52-68.

9. Ruble TL. Effects of actor and observer on attributions of causality in situations of success and failure. *J Soc Psychology* 1973;90:41-44.

10. Ender PB, Bohart AC. Attributions of success and failure. *Psychological Rep* 1974;35:275-278.

11. Weiner B, Russell D, Lerman D. Affective consequences of causal ascriptions. In: Harvey JH, Ickes WJ, Kidd RF, eds. *New Directions in Attributional Research*, Vol. 2. Hillsdale, NJ: Erlbaum, 1976:59-90.

12. Robinson D. From drinking to alcoholism: A sociological commentary. New York: Wiley, 1976.

13. McHugh M. Causal explanations of male and female alcoholics. Paper presented at the Annual Meeting of the Midwestern Psychological Association, 1977.

14. Vuchinich RE, Tucker JA, Bordini E, Sullwold AF. Attributions to causality for drinking behavior made by alcoholics and by normal drinkers. *Drug and Alcohol Dependence* 1981;8:201-206.

15. Gregory D. Indian alcoholism programs in Oklahoma. *Alcohol Technical Reports* 1975;4:37-41.

16. Indian Health Service Task Force on Alcoholism. Alcoholism: A High Priority Health Problem. Department of Health, Education and Welfare, Washington, D.C., 1970.

17. Segal J. (ed.) Research in the Service of Mental Health: Report of the Research Task Force of the National Institute of Mental Health. Rockville, MD: NIMH, 1975.

18. Brod TM. Alcoholism as a mental health problem of Native Americans. *Arch Gen Psychiatry* 1975;32:1385-1391.

19. Stratton R, Zeiner A, Paredes A. Tribal affiliation and prevalence of alcohol problems. *J Stud Alcohol* 1978;39:1166-1177.

20. Jones-Saumty D, Hochhaus L, Dru R, Zeiner AR. Psychological factors of familial alcoholism in American Indians and Caucasians. *J Clin Psychology* 1983;39:783-790.

21. Jones-Saumty DJ, Zeiner AR. Drinking behavior and psychological factors in Indians and Caucasians. *Alc: Clin Exp Res* 1982;6(1):159.

22. Cahalan D, Cisin IH, Crossley HM. American drinking practices: A national survey of behavior and attitudes. Monograph #6. New Brunswick: Rutgers Center for Alcohol Studies, 1969.

# Influence of Family and Religion on Long-term Outcomes Among Opioid Addicts

John J. Hater, PhD
B. Krisna Singh, PhD
D. Dwayne Simpson, PhD

**ABSTRACT.** This study investigated whether family, religion, and personal background variables were related to long-term follow-up outcomes after treatment for drug abuse. The sample consisted of 1,174 opioid addicts admitted to community treatment agencies during 1972-1973 and who were relocated and interviewed in 1978-1979. The results indicated that family and personal background variables made unique contributions to the prediction of a follow-up composite outcome (representing drug use, employment, and criminality) and a general well-being measure. Religion variables accounted for significant and unique variance only in the general well-being variable. The results favor the inclusion of family and religion variables in the scientific explanation of long-term follow-up outcomes among opioid addicts.

Previous research based on the Drug Abuse Reporting Program (DARP) has shown that personal background variables (such as criminal history), during-treatment performance, and length of time spent in treatment are associated with posttreatment outcomes.[1-4]

John J. Hater is an Industrial Psychologist with the Federal Express Corporation, Memphis, TN 38194. B. Krisna Singh is Director, Department of Planning & Development, Richmond Public Schools, Richmond, VA 23219. D. Dwayne Simpson is Professor in the Department of Psychology, Texas A&M University, College Station, TX 77843.

The present research was carried out while the authors were at the Institute of Behavioral Research, Texas Christian University, and the contributions of Dr. S. B. Sells are gratefully acknowledged. This work was supported by the National Institute on Drug Abuse grant H81 DA 01598 as part of a nationally-oriented research program that began in 1968. The interpretations and conclusions presented do not necessarily represent the position of NIDA or the Department of Health and Human Services.

Other drug abuse treatment episodes during the post-DARP follow-up period are also directly associated with improved outcomes, and there are other important influences believed to exist which have not been studied systematically in the DARP research.[5] In particular, family relations and religion of individuals have been implicated as factors that may be involved in drug abuse and treatment outcomes.

The interest in family variables stems from the proposition that the abuse of illicit drugs is not independent of family life influences.[6] Overall, the literature suggests that greater family resources (e.g., greater support and cohesion) tend to be associated with less drug abuse and better psychological well-being, while family disturbances (e.g., family break-up and conflicts) tend to be related to less favorable outcomes.[7-14]

Religious variables represent another potentially important area, and in the substance abuse literature they generally have been conceptualized as a reflection of traditional socialization that imparts conventional norms.[9] Religious variables have been defined in various ways, including membership, religious upbringing, attendance at religious events, and self-described religious commitment. Such measures of presumed religious influence have been shown to be related to abstention or low-level use of illicit drugs.[9,12,15,16]

Information on family and religion was obtained as part of the long-term follow-up research based on the DARP and represents the focus of the present study. In particular, outcomes on drug use, criminality, employment, and general well-being are studied an average of 6 years after admission to DARP treatment (and over 4 years after its termination) in relation to family and religion measures, as well as other personal background variables. A general hypothesis for the present study was that family factors which reflected resources available to the drug user would be positively related to favorable follow-up outcomes, to the extent that they served as a means for coping with drug addiction. Alternatively, family variables that represent sources of disturbance in the family were expected to be related to unfavorable follow-up outcomes based on the assumption that family disturbances create stress which often precedes or maintains drug abuse. For purposes of testing these hypotheses, the previously cited research suggested marriage as well as high scores on parental socioeconomic status, positive psychological support by the family, family contact, and free time spent with family as family *resource* variables, and broken home and high family conflict as family *disturbance* variables.

With regard to religion variables, the literature suggested that more frequent attendance at religious services during childhood, membership in an organized religion, more frequent attendance at religious events as an adult, and greater self-reported religious commitment would be positively associated with favorable follow-up outcomes. This prediction relies on the assumption that religious variables (whether or not they refer to experiences before or after treatment) reflect greater socialization and internalization of conventional norms and thus, a propensity averse to deviant behavior including use and abuse of illicit drugs.

In summary, this study examines the relationships between family and religion variables and long-term follow-up outcomes. Tests of significance are conducted to determine whether family or religion variables account for variance in follow-up outcomes over and above that explained by personal background variables.

## METHOD

### Subjects

A stratified random sample of 2,295 former clients was selected from 26 treatment agencies across the United States for the follow-up study from 16,729 total admissions in Cohort 3 of the DARP.[17] The fieldwork, carried out by the National Opinion Research Center during 1978 and 1979, resulted in the location and completion of 1,496 usable follow-up interviews (65% of the target sample of 2,295 clients). The remaining clients either could not be located (23%), were deceased (5%), refused to participate (5%), or were eliminated for other miscellaneous reasons (2%). Comparisons based on DARP admission and during-treatment records showed that the exclusion of these clients from the research resulted in minimal bias in the completed sample.[18]

The present study was based on a subsample of 1,174 opioid addicts, defined as persons with a history of daily (illicit) use of any natural or synthetic opiate drug prior to treatment in the DARP. As summarized in Table 1, they had an average age at the time of the follow-up of 31 years (standard deviation of 6.7 and range of 20 to 68); they were 59% Black and 41% White and 59% male. Daily opioid use during the last 2 months before DARP admission was reported by 84%; 12% reported less-than-daily opioid use and 4%, no

TABLE 1

Description of Sample (N=1,174)

---

Age:

| | | |
|---|---|---|
| Mean (S.D.) | 31 (6.7) | |
| Range | 20 to 68 | |

Sex:

| | | |
|---|---|---|
| Male | 59% | |
| Female | 41% | |

Race:

| | | |
|---|---|---|
| Black | 59% | |
| White | 41% | |

Opioid Use in 2 Months Before Admission to Treatment:

| | | |
|---|---|---|
| Daily use | 84% | |
| Less-than-daily use | 12% | |
| No use | 4% | |

Other Drug Use 2 Months Before Admission to Treatment:

| | | |
|---|---|---|
| Any marijuana use | 57% | |
| Daily marijuana use | 28% | |
| Any other nonopioid use[a] | 59% | |

Type of Treatment Received:

| | | |
|---|---|---|
| Methadone maintenance | 33% | |
| Therapeutic community | 27% | |
| Outpatient drug free | 21% | |
| Outpatient detoxification | 11% | |
| Intake only | 8% | |

---

[a]Including barbiturates, stimulants, cocaine, hallucinogens, and other drugs.

use. Some use of nonopioid drugs (not counting marihuana) was indicated by 59% of the sample, and 57% used marihuana (including 20% who used it daily). The type of treatment received in the DARP included 33% in methadone maintenance, 27% in therapeutic communities, 21% in outpatient drug-free programs, and 11% in outpatient detoxification; 8% were in a comparison (but not control) group that completed intake/admission procedures but did not return to receive treatment in DARP.

## Follow-up Interview

Confidential follow-up interviews were conducted face-to-face by trained interviewers, and the respondents were each paid 10 dollars for their participation. The interview focused on outcome behaviors (e.g., employment, criminality, drug use) and included background information on family and religion. The outcome behaviors were recorded retrospectively on a month-by-month basis from the time the respondent left the DARP treatment program to the time of the follow-up interview. This interview was conducted at 6 years after admission (on the average) to DARP treatment and covered an average of over 4 years after termination from DARP treatment. In the follow-up studies of previous DARP cohorts, checks for internal consistency and comparisons of self-report information with criminal justice records of post-DARP incarcerations and treatment reentry records indicated a high level of reliability and validity of the data.[19]

## Variables

The analyses completed in this study employed four types of measures. The first involved follow-up outcomes defined on the basis of the last 1-year period immediately preceding the follow-up interview; these served as the dependent measures. These outcome measures were examined with respect to three types of predictor variables—client personal background, family influences, and religion. These measures are described below.

*Outcome measures. General well-being* and a *composite outcome score* were employed as the dependent measures. General well-being reflected the responses to the question, "How have you been feeling in general during the past year?" (scored 1 = in very low spirits, 2 = in low spirits mostly, ..., to 6 = in excellent spirits).

The composite outcome score was based on a sum of the scores for five individual criterion measures (coefficient alpha was .58); the five measures were as follows. *Opioid use* (heroin, illegal methadone, or other opiates) and *nonopioid use* (cocaine, amphetamines, barbiturates or sedatives, hallucinogens, and inhalants, but not including marihuana) reflected the highest frequency of use during any month at risk (i.e., not in a jail, hospital, or residential treatment program) in the last year before the follow-up interview (scored 1 = daily use, 2 = less-than-daily use, and 3 = no use). *Alcohol use* (beer, wine, and liquor consumption converted to a common metric of 80-proof liquor equivalent) was calculated by averaging daily alcohol consumption during the last year for the months at risk (scored 1 = over 8.0 oz., 2 = 4.1 to 8.0 oz., and 3 = 4.0 oz. or less per day). *Productive activities* reflected the proportion of months (at risk) during the last year before follow-up for which the individual was either employed full or part-time, attending school, or engaged in homemaking (scored 1 = 0%, 2 = 1-66%, and 3 = 67-100%). *Crime index* was scored on a 3-point index, taking into account sources of illegal support or reasons for incarceration: 1 = illegal support from robbery, burglary, or dealing drugs, or arrested for crimes against persons or crimes of profit, 2 = illegal support or arrested for so-called "victimless" crimes, such as prostitution and gambling, and 3 = no arrests or illegal support.

*Personal background variables.* Personal background information was obtained from each client at the time of admission to DARP treatment. Except for *age, race,* and *sex,* the personal background variables which are employed in the present study represent composite index measures based on extensive scaling and cluster analyses of the client admission data.[20] *Drug involvement* represented the "hardness" (i.e., opioid drugs as the high extreme and marihuana the low extreme) of the first drug ever used and the first drug ever used daily. *Age at involvement* was based on age-related variables concerning initial drug use and criminal involvement. *Criminal history* reflected the number of arrests, number of convictions, and the total time spent in jail. *Employment record* represented the amount of time employed and the type of work before admission to DARP treatment. *Legal involvement* indicated the client's legal status at admission and pressure from a legal source for treatment. *Educational level* was based on the client's educational attainment in years.

*Family variables.* The family variables consisted of two background index measures developed from admission data and five measures obtained at the time of follow-up.[20] The background measures consisted of *childhood family disruption* which was based on the marital status of the client's parents and who was principally responsible for raising the client and *parental SES* which primarily reflected the relative educational and occupational level of the client's parents. *Marital status* indicated whether the client was married or living as married at the time of follow-up. *Family support* was a composite index based on a sum of (standardized) scores on five items dealing with the degree to which the client reported his/her family was supportive, discouraged drug use, provided help to stop using drugs (2 items), and provided help for other kinds of problems (e.g., legal, alcohol) (coefficient alpha was .69). *Family conflict* reflected how often the client reported having arguments with family members about his/her way of life. *Family contact* was based on summed responses to items concerning how often the client had contact with nine different categories of family members or relatives. *Free time with family* represented how much of a client's free time was spent with his/her family.

*Religious variables.* The religion variables consisted of four single item measures that were asked in the follow-up interview. *Childhood attendance* reflected how often the client attended religious services before 12 years old. *Current membership* was based on whether a client was currently (i.e., at follow-up) a member of an organized religious group. *Current attendance* described how often a client attended religious services at the time of follow-up. *Religious commitment* was measured by the response to the question, "Not counting membership or attendance at religious services, how religious do you consider yourself to be?"

## RESULTS

Since persons included in the present study received different types of treatment during their tenure in the DARP (and some, the intake-only clients, had no treatment at all in the DARP), the relationship between DARP treatment and long-term outcomes was examined first. Analysis of variance was used to compare composite outcome scores in the last year before the follow-up interview and general well-being for persons in DARP methadone maintenance, therapeutic community, outpatient drug free, and outpatient detoxification treatment groups, as well as the intake-only clients. The results showed that there were no statistically significant ($p > .05$) between-group differences in these outcome measures (in contrast to results for the first year immediately after DARP treatment). In addition, the relationships among prediction and outcome variables—as reported below—were the same within each treatment group. The results reported in this study are therefore based on all DARP treatment groups combined.

In order to test the central issue of whether family or religion variables accounted for unique variance in follow-up outcomes, commonality analysis (using hierarchical regression analyses) was employed for the composite outcome and well-being dependent variables.[21] For example, in one set of analyses, personal background and religion variables were first entered into a regression equation and then family variables were entered into the regression equation in a separate step. Tests of statistical significance of the resulting change in the multiple correlation indicated if the set of family variables added significantly and uniquely to the prediction of the outcome measure. Comparable procedures were also followed to determine whether the religion variables as well as the personal background variables accounted for unique variance in follow-up outcomes.

Table 2 shows that multiple correlations of the *composite outcome* score with the different sets of predictor variables were .24 ($p < .01$) for the personal background variables, .23 ($p < .01$) for the family variables, .07 (ns) for the religion variables, and .33 ($p < .01$) for all predictor variables combined (based on clients with no missing data, $N = 1,046$). Significance tests associated with commonality analysis indicated that personal background and family variables, but not religion variables, added significantly and uniquely to the prediction of the composite score ($p < .01$).

Specific variables in each predictor set were examined using significance tests on the regression coefficients (taken from the regression equation that included all variables), and the following variables were found to have significant weights: age at involvement ($p < .05$), criminal history ($p < .01$), marital status ($p < .05$), family conflict ($p < .01$), and free time with family ($p < .01$). For each of the significant family variables, the direction of the relationship was as expected; married status and more free time with family were associated with favorable composite outcome scores, while greater family conflict was associated with unfavorable outcome scores. Although no hypotheses were proposed for the personal background variables, these results were similar to previous DARP findings and indicated that higher age at involvement was positively related to favorable outcomes and a greater criminal history was negatively related to favorable outcomes.

With respect to predictions of the *general well-being* measure, multiple correlations were .20 ($p < .01$) for personal background, .23 ($p < .01$) for family, .14 ($p < .01$) for religion, and .32

TABLE 2

Summary of Results

| Predictor Variables | Composite Outcome | | General Well-Being | |
|---|---|---|---|---|
| | r | β | r | β |
| **Personal Background:** | | | | |
| Age | -.04 | .00 | .00 | .02 |
| Race | .05 | .07 | .02 | .00 |
| Sex | .10** | .06 | -.12** | -.13** |
| Drug involvement | -.01 | -.02 | -.03 | -.02 |
| Age at involvement | .15** | .09* | .07* | .05 |
| Criminal history | -.20** | -.14** | -.08** | -.09* |
| Employment record | .08** | .04 | .10** | .06 |
| Legal involvement | -.05 | .02 | -.06* | -.04 |
| Educational level | .08** | .04 | .01 | -.04 |
| Multiple Correlation (R) | .24** | | .20** | |
| **Family Variables:** | | | | |
| Childhood family disruption | -.05 | -.04 | -.04 | .00 |
| Parental SES | .04 | -.01 | .09** | .09** |
| Marital status | .10** | .07* | .15** | .13** |
| Family support | .08** | .05 | .10** | .08* |
| Family conflict | -.08** | -.11** | -.09** | -.09** |
| Family contact | .09** | .03 | .08** | .03 |
| Free time with family | .18** | .14** | .09** | .03 |
| Multiple Correlation | .23** | | .23** | |
| **Religion Variables:** | | | | |
| Childhood attendance | .01 | .00 | -.02 | -.04 |
| Current membership | .06 | .00 | .05 | .00 |
| Current attendance | .06 | .04 | .04 | .01 |
| Religious commitment | .03 | .01 | .13** | .12** |
| Multiple Correlation (R) | .07 | | .14** | |
| **Combination of All Predictor Sets:** | | | | |
| Multiple Correlation (R) | .33** | | .32** | |

*p < .05
**p < .01

($p < .01$) for all predictor variables combined ($N = 1,046$). Each of the three predictor sets added significantly and uniquely to the prediction of well-being ($p < .01$). The specific variables which had significant regression coefficients consisted of sex ($p < .01$), criminal history ($p <$  .05), parental SES ($p < .01$), marital status ($p < .01$), family support ($p < .05$), family conflict ($p < .01$), and religious commitment ($p < .01$). Direction of the relationships for these significant family and religion variables was as expected; higher parental SES, marital status, greater family support, and greater religious commitment were associated with higher well-being, while greater family conflict was associated with less well-being. The significant personal background variables suggested that females and those with greater criminal history reported less well-being.

## DISCUSSION

The primary objective of this study was to assess whether the predictor sets of personal background, family, and religion variables were associated with unique variance in long-term follow-up outcomes among a treatment sample of opioid addicts. The results indicated that many of the expected relationships were confirmed. The findings were most limited with respect to the religion variables since they accounted for significant and unique variance only in the general well-being measure. Nevertheless, the relationship between religion and well-being was consistent with research which suggests that more religious individuals tend to be more satisfied with life than nonreligious individuals.[24-28] .The lack of association with the composite outcome measure (representing drug use, employment, and criminality) suggested that religion variables in the present study might not have adequately tapped the  internalization of conventional norms opposed to deviant behavior. However, it did appear that religion (measured as religious commitment) represented a positive predictor for at least the "emotional affect" (i.e., well-being) of opioid addicts at follow-up.

With regard to the results for the personal background and family variables, the results indicated that each set of these predictors was significantly and uniquely related to general well-being as well as the composite outcome score. These findings for the personal background variables were consistent with previous DARP research on follow-up outcomes, particularly concerning the negative implications of criminal history on favorable outcomes.[3,4,23] The specific findings for the family variables were consistent with the hypothesis that greater family resources (e.g., greater support) would be positively related to favorable outcomes, while family disturbances (e.g., conflicts) would be negatively related to favorable outcomes. The results are similar to findings in prior research even though they were based on dissimilar samples, criteria, or types of abused substances compared to those in the present study.[7,10]

However, the research was unable to address whether family variables such as family support and family conflict contributed to follow-up outcomes or were a result of outcomes. For example, clients with low family conflict may have more favorable follow-up outcomes but they may have low family conflict because they have favorable outcomes. Investigations employing a design that incorporates the examination of reciprocal causation between family variables and outcomes are necessary to answer this question.[29]

Finally, it should be stressed that although the findings of the present study were generally positive with respect to the implied contributions of family and religious variables to outcome, the actual amount of variance involved in the associations was small (i.e., under 10%, as indicated by the squared multiple correlations). Further refinement and development of the measures representing these variables might raise the magnitude of the relationships observed. Nevertheless, investigations of long-term outcomes and adjustments of individuals (especially opioid addicts) have frequently ignored the dynamic familial context and religion, and the present study asserts the importance of considering such measures in the scientific explanation of such outcomes.

# REFERENCES

1. Simpson DD, Sells SB. Effectiveness of treatment for drug abuse: an overview of the DARP research program. Advances in Alcohol & Substance Abuse. 1982; 2(1):7-29.

2. Simpson DD. The relation of time spent in drug abuse treatment to posttreatment outcome. Am J Psych. 1979; 136:1449-53.

3. Simpson DD, Savage LJ, Lloyd ML. Follow-up evaluation of treatment of drug abuse during 1969 to 1972. Arch Gen Psych. 1979; 36:772-80.

4. Simpson DD, Savage LJ, Sells SB. Evaluation of outcomes in the first year after drug abuse treatment: a replication study based on 1972-1973 DARP admissions. National Technical Information Service, U.S. Department of Commerce, Springfield, VA, 1981. Document No. PB 81-128076.

5. Simpson DD, Savage LJ. Drug abuse treatment readmissions and outcomes. Arch Gen Psych. 1980; 37:896-901.

6. Blechman EA. Conventional wisdom about familial contributions to substance abuse. Am J Drug & Alc Abuse. 1982; 9(1):35-53.

7. Bromet E. Moos RH. Environmental resources and the posttreatment functioning of alcohol patients. Journal of Health and Social Behavior. 1977; 18:326-38.

8. Cronkite RC, Moos RH. Evaluating alcoholism treatment programs: an integrated approach. J Consult & Clin Psych, 1978; 46:1105-19.

9. Gorsuch RL, Butler MC. Initial drug abuse: a review of predisposing social psychological factors. Psych Bull. 1976; 83:120-37.

10. Graeven DB, Schaef RD. Family life and levels of involvement in adolescent heroin epidemic. The International J of the Addictions, 1978; 13:747-71.

11. Harbin HT, Mazian HM. The family of drug abusers: a literature review. Family Process, 1975; 14:411-31.

12. Penk W, Robinowitz R, Kidd R, Nisle A. Perceived family environments among ethnic groups of compulsive heroin users. Addictive Behaviors, 1979; 4:279-309.

13. Seldin NE. The family of the addict: a review of the literature. The International J of the Addictions, 1972; 7:97-107.

14. Stanton MD, Todd TC, Heard DB, Kirschner S, Kleiman JI, Mowatt DT, Riley P, Scott SM, Van Deusen JM. Heroin addiction as a family phenomenon: a new conceptual model. Am J Drug & Alc Abuse, 1978; 5:125-50.

15. Daum M, Lavenhar MA. Religiosity and drug use: a study of Jewish and Gentile college students. NIDA Services Research Report, Washington, D. C.: U.S. Government Printing Office, 1980. Document No. ADM80-939.

16. Turner CJ, Willis RG. The relationship between self-reported religiosity and drug use by college students. J of Drug Education, 1979; 9:67-78.

17. Simpson DD, Lloyd MR, Savage LJ. Sample design and data collection for the follow-up study of 1972-1973 DARP admissions. Texas Christian University, Institute of Behavioral Research, Forth Worth, Report 79-14, 1979.

18. Simpson DD, Lloyd MR, Sells SB. Nonresponse bias in the follow-up sample of 1972-1973 DARP admissions. Texas Christian University Institute of Behavioral Research, Fort Worth, Report 79-16, 1979.

19. Simpson DD, Lloyd MR, Gent MJ. Reliability and validity of data: National follow-up study of admissions to drug abuse treatments in the DARP during 1969-1972. Texas Christian University, Institute of Behavioral Research, Forth Worth, Report 76-18, 1976.

20. Joe GW. Patient background indices for a drug-abusing population. In: S. B. Sells, ed, Studies of the effectiveness of treatments for drug abuse, Vol. 2, Research on patients, treatments and outcomes. Cambridge, MA; Ballinger Publishing Company, 1974.

21. Kerlinger FN, Pedhazer EJ. Multiple regression in behavioral research. Holt, Rinehart, and Winston, New York, 1973.

22. Sells SB, Simpson DD. eds, The effectiveness of drug abuse treatment. Vols. 3-5, Cambridge, MA: Ballinger Publishing Company, 1976.

23. Simpson DD, Savage LJ, Lloyd ML, Sells SB. Evaluation of drug abuse treatments based on first year follow-up. NIDA Services Research Monograph, Washington, D.C.: U.S. Government Printing Office. 1978; Document No. ADM 78-701.

24. Clemente F, Sauer WJ. Life satisfaction in the United States. Social Forces, 1976; 54:621-31.

25. Gurin G, Veroff J, Feld S. Americans view their mental health. Ann Arbor, MI, University of Michigan Press, 1960.

26. Hadaway CK. Life satisfaction and religion: a reanalysis. Social Forces, 1978; 57:636-43.

27. McCann RV. The churches and mental health. New York: Basic Books, 1962.

28. Singh BK, Williams JS. Satisfaction with health and physical condition among the elderly. J Psych Treatment & Evaluation, 1982; 4:403-08.

29. James LR, Singh BK. An introduction to the logic, assumption, and basic analytic procedures of two-stage least squares. Psych Bull, 1978; 85:1104-22.

# Women, Alcohol, and Sexuality

Stephanie S. Covington, PhD
Janet Kohen, PhD

**ABSTRACT.** Neither women's sexuality nor their alcohol use has been studied until recently. Research on the relationship between the two has been even more neglected. While the literature has acknowledged that sexual dysfunction and abuse may coexist with women's alcoholism, the possibility that these may predate or lead to excessive alcohol use has not been investigated. This study explores sexual experience, dysfunction, and abuse among 35 alcoholic women and their paired nonalcoholic counterparts. Results suggest that both dysfunction and abuse may precede as well as accompany alcoholism. The findings indicate that issues of sexuality should be included in recovery programs for women because alcohol and sexual experience are linked in most of these alcoholic women's lives.

Although the number of women who drink has doubled since World War II and the number of female alcoholics has correspondingly increased,[1] only in the past decade has the female alcoholic received much research attention.[2] Prior to that she was either ignored or assumed to be affected by the same etiology and treatment as the male alcoholic. A parallel exists in the field of research on female sexuality. Until recently there has been relatively little information available on female sexuality. What did exist was the product of male researchers, representing the male interpretation of how women should feel and behave. As a result of the neglect of women in both fields, only a handful of studies have investigated sexuality in the lives of alcoholic women. As Carpenter

---

Stephanie Covington is a Consultant/Trainer and Clinician in Private Practice, La Jolla, California. Janet Kohen is with the Women's Studies Department, San Diego State University. For reprints, contact: Stephanie S. Covington, PhD, 1129 Torrey Pines Road, La Jolla, CA 92037.

*41*

and Armenti noted, "Most experts comment on human sexual behavior and alcohol as though only males drink and have sexual interests."[3] The consequences are evident in treatment programs, most of which virtually ignore sexual dysfunction as an issue in the recovery of alcoholic women.[4]

Neglect of the relationship of female sexuality and alcoholism is surprising since throughout most of human history sexuality and alcohol have been related in various cultures.[5] While the relationship between the two is often based on questionable, if not incorrect beliefs, the relationship is nonetheless a primary one. Sexuality, according to sex therapist Helen Singer Kaplan, is the integration of the biological, emotional, and spiritual aspects of one's self.[6] Alcohol affects all these aspects of a person as well. Since one's sexuality is the expression of who one is and how one relates to others, alcohol use affects one of the most fundamental expressions of self.

## ALCOHOL AND FEMALE SEXUALITY

The relationship between women's sexuality and their alcohol use is a function of the social position of women within the society. Women's socialization and the norms that govern their adult behavior have defined the boundaries between acceptable and unacceptable expression of women's sexual and drinking behaviors. These boundaries and the cultural ideas that determine the form for expressing these two areas of human life are considerably different for women than for men. Passive or limited interest in both are valued for women while almost the opposite is true for men.[1,7] Quantity in both often brings respect for the man but distain for the woman. While both alcohol use and sexual interest have become more permissible for women in recent years, excess in either area results in more extreme and more negative disapproval for women than men.[8]

These two areas of female behavior are not just parallel in form of expected behavior and reaction to it, they are also interrelated. The salience of the relationship is expressed in one of the bases for extreme disapproval of intoxicated women. Such women are commonly viewed as sexually "promiscuous."[1] Thus, negative reaction to the alcoholic woman compounds disapproval of her drinking with disapproval of her presumed excessive sexual interest. This disapproval can be expressed in a variety of ways. One is physical abuse, and alcoholic women report a high incidence of battering and abuse.[9,10]

The cultural link between alcohol use and sexual expression by women has been formalized within academic literature. The disinhibition hypothesis is the prevailing view of how alcohol enhances sexual activity. As a central nervous system depressant, alcohol is theorized to depress higher brain functions that inhibit sexual behavior, thus reducing anxiety and fear.[6] Several studies have documented women's subjective experience of increased sexual enjoyment when drinking.[11,12] However, physiological research contradicts women's subjective response. With alcohol ingestion, women's physiological sexual arousal has been found to decrease and latency to orgasm has been found to increase. The women themselves also report increased difficulty of attaining orgasm and decrease in intensity of orgasm.[13,14]

The disinhibition hypothesis fails to account for these physiological findings. Social learning may better explain the discrepancy between women's subjective and their physiological sexual response.

If a woman learns to associate drinking with sex, this attitude leads her to expect that drinking will enhance her sexual enjoyment. Even though her sexual response is depressed, she can still interpret the sexual activity as enjoyable. However, this explanation may not fully explain the relationship between subjective and physiological sexual response for the chronic women drinker.

Research indicates not just a decrease in the sexual functioning of the chronic woman drinker but serious sexual dysfunction. Whitfield et al.[4] reviewed clinical studies of alcohol and sexual dysfunction and listed a variety of physiological mechanisms induced by alcohol abuse that can produce·impaired sexual functioning. In a study by Sholty,[15] 67% of the alcoholic women in the sample reported their orgasmic experience had deteriorated after their drinking became a problem and 47% became anorgasmic. In studies of alcoholic women by Beckman[12] and Pinhas,[16] in which comparison groups of nonalcoholic women were used, alcoholic women reported a higher level of generalized sexual dissatisfaction than their matched nonalcoholic controls. These latter two studies did not identify when sexual dysfunction began for these women relative to their drinking careers.

Because alcohol is frequently used as a means of coping with stressful life situations, identifying whether drinking problems or sexual difficulties came first becomes an important issue. Unfortunately, data on sexual dysfunction among problem drinking women often suffer from methodological limitations. Definitions of alcoholism and sexual dysfunction are often vague, and terminology such as "frigidity" and "promiscuity" reflects moral judgments and sexual stereotypes. Nevertheless, some research does suggest sexual dysfunction as a precipitating factor in alcohol abuse. Kinsey,[17] for instance, found that 72% of alcoholic women had a history of "frigidity." A number of investigators have found that women alcoholics identify marital problems, often including sexual difficulties, as initial reason for their problem drinking.[18,19,20,21]

The same question of time order can be raised with regard to alcohol use and abuse experienced by problem drinking women. Earlier, abuse was suggested as a reaction to the intoxicated woman. However, a personal history of abuse may also be a precipitating factor in the lives of alcoholic women. Research on abuse among alcoholic women, like that on sexual dysfunction, offers few clues as to when the problem began. Some findings have suggested that abuse may precede drinking problems. Assuming that incest is concentrated among the young, several researchers have reported that 40-50% of the alcoholic women in their sample were incest victims.[22,23] Scott[24] reported that 70% of the study sample of battered wives were frequent drinkers.

Whether the abuse occurred before or after the onset of problem drinking, there is a relationship between abuse and sexual difficulties. It is highly obvious from accumulated data on physical and sexual abuse that there are gender differences between the victims and the perpetrators of this violence. In general, men are the perpetrators and women are the victims. Often women are in close relationships with the men who abuse them, generating feelings of fear and distrust toward men. As a result, whenever the abuse occurs in the alcoholic woman's life, it is bound to affect her heterosexual relationships. The relationship between rape and later sexual dysfunction[10] is a concrete example of possible long-term consequences.

To begin to provide the answers to some of these questions requires research that compares the alcoholic to the nonalcoholic woman in order to establish whether abuse and sexual dysfunction are experienced in greater frequency in the lives of the alcoholic woman. Large random sample surveys of women or longitudinal studies would provide the most accurate data on which to base answers. While the following study has neither one of these two designs, it does address some of the issues raised above and begins to suggest some answers and some additional questions for future research.

## THE STUDY

*Method and sample.* The following study was an examination of sexual experience, sexual dysfunction, and physical and sexual abuse from questionnaire responses gathered from 35 alcoholic women and 35 paired nonalcoholic women. Reports of sexual experience and dysfunction prior to and during the alcoholic drinking phase were also obtained from the alcoholic sample. Age of abuse and length of time it occurred by relationship of the perpetrator to the participant were requested from both the alcoholic and the nonalcoholic samples.

The alcoholic group consisted of Caucasian women who were volunteers from recovery programs which included Alcoholics Anonymous, alcohol recovery homes, and hospital treatment programs in San Diego and Orange Counties, California. These women were assessed as alcoholic by their participation in a treatment program and not by clinical diagnosis. The nonalcoholic group came from the same geographical regions and each participant was paired with her alcoholic counterpart by age, education, marital status, and religious background. Matches were obtained through advertisements in newspapers and notices at businesses, educational institutions, and public service agencies. After establishing the respondent as a match for one of the alcoholic sample of women, she was screened using the Mortimer-Filkens Screening Test[25] to determine that she was not a problem drinker. If she was accepted, she was given a questionnaire. Characteristics of the matched pairs in the sample are given in Table 1.

As can be seen from Table 1, the typical woman in the sample was in her late 30's, having an educational background of some college. However, the sample ranged from women as young as 19 to those as old as 68, and their educational attainment ranged from grade school to advanced graduate degrees. Over two-thirds of the women were employed, and their positions ranged from service workers to professional occupations. Forty-three percent were married or cohabiting. Of the remaining 20 women, 11 were no longer

Table 1

Characteristics of Sample Matched Pairs

(N = 35)

| | Matched Pairs |
|---|---|
| Current Age | % |
| 19-29 | 22.9 |
| 30-39 | 28.5 |
| 40-49 | 31.5 |
| 50+ | 17.1 |
| Level of Education Achieved* | |
| Less than high school graduate | 8.6 |
| High school graduage | 25.7 |
| Some college (or more) | 65.7 |
| Current Marital Status* | |
| Single | 25.7 |
| Divorced, separated, widowed | 31.5 |
| Married (or cohabiting) | 42.8 |
| Religious Background* | |
| Roman Catholic | 28.6 |
| Protestant | 68.6 |
| Jew | 2.9 |

*Exact match achieved.

married with only 1 woman widowed, and 9 were single. Most of
the women were Protestant, but the sample included 10 Catholics
and 1 Jewish woman.

The alcoholic women were newly recovering, having remained
sober from 3 to 12 months with an average length of sobriety of 7½
months. They had been drinking alcoholically from 1 to 25 years

with the average being 9½ years. During alcoholism, 20 reported their sexual orientation as heterosexual, 13 as bisexual, and 2 as lesbian.

The statistical techniques used to assess significance of differences between the two paired samples consisted of the McNemar test for significance of changes and the Wilcoxon matched pairs signed-ranks test.

*Sexual experience.* To assess sexual experience, the respondents were asked whether they had engaged in any of seven different sexual activities ranging from intercourse to sadomasochism. Table 2

Table 2

A Comparison of the Variety of Sexual Experiences

Reported by Alcoholic and Nonalcoholic

Women

| | Alcoholic (N = 34) | Nonalcoholic (N = 35) |
|---|---|---|
| | % | % |
| Orgasm | 85 | 80 |
| Masturbation | 82 | 71 |
| Intercourse | 97 | 69 |
| Manual stimulation (by partner) | 92 | 63 |
| Oral stimulation | 88 | 57 |
| Vibrator | 38 | 26 |
| Anal intercourse | 32 | 9 |
| Sadomasochism | -- | -- |
| Other | -- | 6 |

Note. N = 34, Wilcoxon Z = 2.38, p ≤ .02

shows that compared to the nonalcoholic women, the alcoholic women reported experiencing a greater variety of sexual activities, such as intercourse plus oral or anal sex (Z = 2.38, $p < .05$). They also reported using alcohol more often with sexual activity (Z = 4.45, $p < .001$), and were more likely to agree that alcohol contributed to good sexual experiences (Z = 2.59, $p < .01$). While the alcoholic women engaged in a wider variety of sexual activities than the nonalcoholic women, their greater usage of alcohol with sex was not associated with reported higher frequency of sex with a partner ($p$ = NS), though they did report engaging in a higher frequency of masturbation (Z = 5.01, $p < .001$).

The lack of differences between the two groups in frequency of sexual activity indicates that the disinhibition hypothesis received only limited support from these data. Alcohol may reduce the anxiety associated with less traditional modes of sexual activity, but among this group of women it did not increase the frequency of sexual activities with a partner.

*Sexual dysfunction.* Sexual dysfunction was measured both generally and specifically. The women were first asked if they had experienced any of a set of six sexual difficulties—from lack of orgasm to vaginismus. Table 3 indicates that the alcoholic women reported significantly more of these dysfunctions than the nonalcoholic women (Z = 2.63, $p < .01$). Three of the six items used as an overall measure of sexual dysfunction were combined to assess general sexual dysfunction as it has usually been defined clinically. Those items included lack of sexual interest, lack of sexual arousal or pleasure, and/or lack of lubrication. Using this more specific measure, the alcoholic women also reported significantly more general sexual dysfunction (Z = 2.27, $p < .05$). Eighty-five percent of the alcoholic women reported sexual dysfunction as compared to 59% of the nonalcoholic women.

Finally, the orgasmic dysfunction of the women was assessed by their response to the question, "Please indicate about how often you were orgasmic when you engaged in sex?" The women could respond in 6 categories with 1 = "about all of the time" to 6 = "never." The alcoholic women reported significantly more orgasmic dysfunction (Z = 1.96, $p < .05$).

Despite the differences on all three measures of sexual dysfunction, sexual dysfunction among the alcoholic group of women cannot be attributed to problem drinking alone. Seventy-nine percent reported having experienced sexual dysfunction before alcoholism,

Table 3

A Comparison of Sexual Dysfunction Reported

by Alcoholic and Nonalcoholic Women

| | Alcoholic (N = 33) % | Nonalcoholic (N = 33) % |
|---|---|---|
| Lack of orgasm | 64 | 27 |
| Lack of sexual interest | 64 | 44 |
| Lack of sexual arousal or pleasure | 61 | 30 |
| Lack of lubrication | 46 | 24 |
| Painful intercourse | 24 | 9 |
| Muscular spasms (Vaginismus) | 6 | -- |

Note.  N = 33, Wilcoxon Z = 2.63, p < .009

85% during alcoholism, and 74% reported continued sexual dysfunction during sobriety. There was no significant difference between before alcoholism and alcoholism periods.

*Abuse.* The women in this study were asked to report all instances of abuse they had experienced in their lifetime. The women reported abuse according to their own definition and were asked to report each instance separately by whether it was physical or sexual, the age at which it occurred, the relationship of the perpetrator to them, the frequency, and the duration of the abusive relationship. The data provided an assessment of both the number of women in each group who had experienced any abuse and the frequency of abusive instances experienced by each group.

Although abuse is a common life experience for both groups of women, more alcoholic than nonalcoholic women reported abuse at some time during their lives. For sexual abuse the difference was significant ($Z = 1.54$, $p = .06$), with 74% of the alcoholic women reporting at least one instance of sexual abuse and 50% of the non-alcoholic women reporting such. The difference was not significant for physical abuse, though it was in the same direction as for sexual abuse. Fifty-two percent of the alcoholic women reported an instance of physical abuse compared to 34% of the nonalcoholic women ($p = .21$).

Summary data descriptive of the instances of abuse experienced by the two groups indicate some similarities and some differences. For both groups the perpetrator of the abuse, whether physical or sexual, was predominately male and known to the woman. Over 90% of the perpetrators of sexual abuse and over three-quarters of the perpetrators of physical abuse reported by both groups were males. Perpetrators of sexual abuse were known to the woman in over 70% of the reported instances and perpetrators of physical abuse were known to the woman in 100% of the reported instances.

While the frequency of sexual abuse was somewhat similar between the alcoholic and the nonalcoholic groups, there were differences in both the type of abuse and the duration.[26] Incest accounted for 34% of the reported cases of sexual abuse among the alcoholic subjects, and rape accounted for 58%. Together, rape and incest accounted for 92% of all instances of reported sexual abuse. Attempted rape and molestation comprised only 8% of all abuse reported by these women. In contrast, 55% of the sexual abuse reported by the nonalcoholic women involved attempted rape (14%) or molestation (41%). While all sexual abuse is traumatic, the data indicated that alcoholic women were more likely to experience the most extreme forms of sexual assault. In addition, only alcoholic women reported sexual abuse with the same perpetrator extending for a period of 10 years or more.

Characteristics of the reported instances of physical abuse are quite similar for the alcoholic and the nonalcoholic women—with one exception. The alcoholic women were more likely to experience chronic physical abuse; that is, abuse at least once a month for a year or more from the same perpetrator. Almost half of these alcoholic women reporting physical abuse, 45%, reported chronic abuse as compared to approximately one of eight, 12% of the nonalcoholic women.

Overall, these data indicated that sexual and physical abuse usually perpetrated by known males were common life experiences for

Table 4

Type of Sexual Abuse by Number of

Women and Instances Reported

|  | Alcoholic (N=35) | | Nonalcoholic (N=35) | |
|---|---|---|---|---|
|  | Women (N=22) | Instances (N=53) | Women (N=17) | Instances (N=37) |
|  | % | % | % | % |
| Incest | 34 | 34 | 17 | 16 |
| Rape | 34 | 58 | 14 | 24 |
| Attempted Rape | 3 | 2 | 12 | 14 |
| Molestation | 9 | 6 | 31 | 41 |
| Other | 0 | 0 | 6 | 5 |

both the alcoholic and the nonalcoholic women. However, alcoholic women experienced more sexual abuse, of a more extreme nature, and were more likely to experience the abuse over a longer period of their lives. They also tended to experience more physical abuse, and the abuse was more likely to have been frequent during the period that it was perpetrated.

While the subjects reported their age at the time when each instance of abuse began, information on the age at which they began to use alcohol was not obtained. Whether alcohol use contributed to abuse, resulted from it, or both could not be answered. However, of the subjects who reported having experienced sexual abuse any time during their lives, all of the alcoholic women reported abuse on or before the age of 10, and 65% of the nonalcoholic group reported abuse by that age ($X^2 = 13.07$, $p < .001$). Over 90% of sexual abuse reported by alcoholic women was rape or incest; therefore, such abuse was likely to be the typical experience prior to their eventual alcohol abuse. Physical abuse displayed a different pattern. For those physically abused, 74% of the alcoholic and 82% of the nonalcoholic women reported their first abuse before age 10 ($p$ = NS).

Table 5

Characteristics of Sexual and Physical Abuse

|  | Sexual Abuse | | Physical Abuse | |
|---|---|---|---|---|
|  | Alc | Nonalc | Alc | Nonalc |
| **Perpetrators** | | | | |
| Sex | | | | |
| Male | 93% | 100% | 83% | 75% |
| Female | 7% | -- | 17% | 25% |
| Known to women | 70% | 86% | 100% | 100% |
|  | N=23 | N=17 | N=19 | N=11 |
| Frequency | | | | |
| Single | 36% | 46% | 13% | 12% |
| Multiple | 48% | 35% | 42% | 75% |
| Chronic* | 16% | 19% | 45% | 12% |
|  | N=22 | N=17 | N=18 | N=11 |
| Duration | | | | |
| Up to 1 year | 55% | 57% | 26% | 19% |
| 1-10 years | 31% | 43% | 45% | 50% |
| 10 years or more | 14% | -- | 29% | 31% |
|  | N=22 | N=17 | N=17 | N=11 |

*Chronic abuse is defined as once a month or more for 1 year or more.

## CONCLUSIONS

Despite the birth of the sexual revolution, women continue to be more inhibited, less receptive, and more passive than men in their sexual activity. Even when they want to be more sexually expressive, the men in their relationships often express dislike when women initiate such expression.[27] Because alcohol is linked to sexual inhibition in our society, its use may reduce anxiety when women experiment with their sexuality. However, women may also use alcohol as an excuse for the guilt or shame they feel when they go beyond the socially defined boundaries for their sexual expression. Thus, alcohol may prevent a woman from accepting her sexual satisfactions, desires, and identity. On a physiological level, alcohol is likely to compound any of the dysfunctions she has experienced in expressing her sexuality in the past.

The findings from this study suggest a spiraling relationship between dysfunction and alcohol use that warrants further research. Sexual dysfunction may start prior to the alcoholic period. Beliefs about alcohol's contribution to a good sexual experience may prompt greater use of alcohol as a means to treat the problem, but the increased intake is likely to simply make the problem worse. Some additional data from this study support this hypothesis. As reported earlier, the alcoholic women were more likely to agree that alcohol contributed to a good sexual experience and to use alcohol more often with sex than the nonalcoholic women. However, they did not report greater satisfaction with sexual responsiveness ($Z = 2.22$, $p < .05$), and they reported less satisfaction with their sexual relations ($Z = 1.95$, $p < .05$).

Sexual abuse early in a woman's life may add to both the probability of her sexual dysfunction and her propensity for alcohol abuse. The higher frequency of both sexual dysfunction and sexual abuse in the lives of the alcoholic women in this study suggests that future research be addressed to the area of alcohol use and these as well as other aspects of women's sexuality. Because the nonalcoholic women did not hold the belief that alcohol would increase their sexual enjoyment but also reported sexual dysfunction, further research on the mediating role of women's belief systems and their use of alcohol as a way of coping with their sexuality seems indicated. The woman who believes that alcohol enhances her sexual pleasure may use it with sexual activity, and vice versa. Any research should address the interactive relationship between women's sexuality and their use of alcohol or other drugs as both a response to and a contributor to their sexual expression.

Although this study involved a relatively small sample, the findings do suggest some implications for treatment settings. Can the posttreatment alcoholic woman become a healthy, functioning individual if the abuse she has experienced or her sexual functioning is not part of the total treatment program? Can either of these issues be addressed in agencies without sufficient female staff or all female treatment groups? At least one study indicates that female alcoholics are more likely to seek treatment in agencies where the percentage of female staff is relatively high.[28] If abuse is not treated within agency programs, can we expect the posttreatment alcoholic woman not to become a contributor to the generational transmission of family violence? If sexuality is not part of the treatment setting, can we expect her to express her sexuality in satisfying relationships during and after her recovery?

Sexuality is an integral aspect of women's lives. It is also linked with alcohol. Issues that are part of the life experience of a woman alcoholic must be addressed if sobriety is to be maintained. Treatment providers need to be aware of women's sexuality, the physiological as well as the socially defined and emotional aspects. Because women's sexual functioning has only recently become a focus of research, treatment providers need initial training in the area, including an assessment of the provider's own sexual attitudes, values, and knowledge. Ongoing education for treatment providers is important for the female patient's total recovery. For example, training should dispel such common myths as "promiscuity" among alcoholic women. Neither the data from this study nor that reported by Schuckit[29] substantiates this commonly held belief. Because most alcoholic women's sexual dysfunction and the abuse they experience in their prealcoholic and alcoholic periods usually involve men and those men are usually known to the women, if not close to them, alcoholic women should be in treatment groups with other women where they can share their experiences and feel safe in doing so.

Finally, just as sexuality must be recognized as part of an alcoholic woman's life, abuse must be recognized as a common and traumatic contributor to her perspective on and response to her future interpersonal relationships. As a victim, she may have learned to accept the role of victim and also be at risk in becoming a perpetrator of abuse in the future.

This study suggests that sexual dysfunction and abuse may both precede and accompany alcohol use. Alcohol may play a role in both alleviating the problems and compounding them. Sobriety may lessen the intensity of the problems but it is unlikely to erase them. Researchers and treatment providers alike need to recognize the relationship between alcohol use, sexuality, and abuse if their goal is to assist in women's development of fulfilling lives in sobriety.

# REFERENCES

1. Gomberg ESL. Historical and political perspective: Women and drug use. J of Social Issues 1982;2:9-24.
2. Beckman LJ. Women alcoholics: A review of social and psychological studies. J of Studies on Alcohol 1975;36(7):797-824.
3. Carpenter JA, Armenti NP. Some effects of ethanol on human sexual and aggressive behavior. In: Kissin B, Belerter H, eds. The biology of alcoholism (vol. 2): Physiology and behavior. New York: Plenum Press, 1972;509.
4. Whitfield CL, Redmond AC, Quinn SJ. Alcohol use, alcoholism, and sexual functioning. Unpublished manuscript, University of Maryland School of Medicine, 1979.
5. Sandmaier M. The invisible alcoholics: Women and alcohol abuse in America. New York: McGraw-Hill, 1980.
6. Kaplan HS. The new sex therapy: Active treatment of sexual dysfunctions. New York: Brunner/Mazel, 1974.
7. Gross AE. The male role and heterosexual behavior. J. of Social Issues 1978;87-107.
8. Hanna E. Attitudes towards problem drinkers. J of Studies of Alcohol 1978;39:98-108.
9. Hindman MH. Family violence. Alcohol, Health and Research World 1979;1:2-11.
10. Hammond DC, Jorgensen GQ, Ridgeway DM. Sexual adjustment of female alcoholics. Unpublished manuscript. Salt Lake City: Alcohol and Drug Abuse Clinic, University of Utah, 1979.
11. Athanasion R, Shaver P, Tavris C. Sex: A Psychology Today report on more than 20,000 responses to 101 questions on sexual attitudes and practices. Psychology Today 1970;4:39-52.
12. Beckman LJ. Reported effects of alcohol on the sexual feelings and behavior of women alcoholics and nonalcoholics. J of Studies on Alcohol 1979;40:272-282.
13. Wilson GT, Lawson DM. Effects of alcohol on sexual arousal in women. J of Abnormal Psychology 1976;85:489-497.
14. Malatesta VJ, Pollack RH, Crotty TD. Alcohol effects on the orgasmic response in human females. Paper presented at the Annual Meeting of the Psychonomic Society, Phoenix, Arizona, November, 1979.
15. Sholty MJ. Female sexual experience and satisfaction as related to alcohol consumption. Unpublished manuscript. Baltimore: Alcohol and Drug Abuse Program, University of Maryland, 1979.
16. Pinhas V. Sex guilt and sexual control in the woman alcoholic in early sobriety. Unpublished doctoral dissertation, Department of Health Education, New York University, 1978.
17. Kinsey BA. The female alcoholic: A social psychological study. Springfield, Illinois: Charles C. Thomas, 1966.
18. Curlee J. Alcoholism and the "empty nest." Bulletin of the Menninger Clinic 1969;33:165-171.
19. Dahlgren L. Female alcoholics: A psychiatric and social study. Stockholm: Karolinska Institute, 1979.
20. Sclare WB. The female alcoholic. British J of Addiction 1970;65:99-107.
21. Tamerin JS. The psychotherapy of alcoholic women. In: Zimberg S, Wallace J, Blume SB, eds. Practical approaches to alcoholism psychotherapy. New York: Plenum, 1978;183-203.
22. Evans S, Schaefer S. Why women's sexuality is important to address in chemical dependency treatment programs. Grassroots 1980;37:37-40.
23. Benward J, Densen-Gerber J. Incest as a causative factor in antisocial behavior: An exploratory study. Contemporary Drug Problems 1975;4:323-340.
24. Scott PD. Battered wives. Brit J of Psychiatry 1974;125:433-441.
25. Jackson GR. The Mortimer-Filkins test: Court procedures for identifying problem drinkers. Alcohol Health Research World 1976;15:852-859.

26. Although 25 alcoholic women reported sexual abuse, only 22 gave complete data on each instance.

27. Rubin L. Women of a certain age. New York: Harper and Row, 1979.

28. Beckman LJ, Kocel KM. The treatment-delivery system and alcohol abuse in women: Social policy implications. J of Social Issues 1982;2:139-152.

29. Schuckit MA. Sexual disturbance in the woman alcoholic. Medical Aspects of Human Sexuality 1972;6:44-65.

# Sex-Role Values and Bias
# in Alcohol Treatment Personnel

Marsha Vannicelli, PhD
Gayle Hamilton, PhD

**ABSTRACT.** During a two day training workshop with 45 alcohol treatment agency personnel, the impact of sex-role bias on clinical practice with alcoholic clients was examined. More specifically, data were gathered on: 1) client comfort level of surrogate clients as related to perceived sex-role values of treatment personnel; and 2) the impact of patient sex and sex-linked characteristics of presenting problems (whether problems are "typically" male or female, and whether "sex-appropriate") on each of the following: perceived importance of client's presenting problems, specificity of the treatment plan to problems presented, and clinician's estimate of client prognosis. The results suggest that sex-role values of treatment personnel influence client comfort, that female clients are seen as having a poorer prognosis than males, and that presenting problems are perceived to be more important if they are sex-appropriate than if they are not sex-appropriate (the least important problems being female problems in a male client).

A growing body of literature documents the presence in Western culture of sex-role stereotypes (consensual norms and beliefs regarding the differential characteristics of men and women) and suggests that these stereotypes have implications for clinical judgments, treatment planning, and psychotherapy. These stereotypes, which data suggest are subtly transmitted beginning a few days after birth,[1] become part of the world view of both male and female therapists—influencing their perceptions of and expectations for

Marsha Vannicelli is Director, Outpatient Service, Appleton Treatment Center, McLean Hospital; and Associate Professor, Harvard University Medical School. Gayle Hamilton is a Consultant and Trainer in Washington, D.C. Address reprints to Marsha Vannicelli, Ph.D., Appleton Treatment Center, 115 Mill Street, Belmont, MA 02178.

*57*

their clients. In fact, there is reason to believe that, in a manner analogous to the initial transmission of sex-role stereotypes, these limited (and limiting) views of "manliness" and "womanliness" are further reinforced by mental health professionals as they help their clients "adjust to reality."[2]

Although a few studies demonstrate the impact of these stereotypes on the behavior of mental health practitioners,[3-7] to our knowledge prior to the program that we shall describe, there were no data available regarding the implications of these stereotypes for the treatment of alcoholic clients. Given the a priori difficulties and stigmata that face the female alcholic when she acknowledges having a stereotypically "male problem", issues of sex-role stereotyping are particularly salient in this population from the outset and need special attention. To address this problem we developed a training and research program designed to help alcohol treatment personnel clarify their own personal sex-role values and to experience directly the effect of these values on the clinical decisions that they make and the messages that they transmit to their alcoholic clients.

In the course of a two-day workshop we examined the impact of sex-role bias on several phases of clinical practice: 1) client comfort level as related to perceived sex-role values of treatment personnel; 2) therapist perceptions of the importance of an alcholic client's presenting problems depending upon: a) sex of the client, b) whether the presenting problems are typically male or female problems, and c) whether the client presents with "sex-appropriate" problems (e.g., male problems in a male client, female problems in a female, rather than vice-versa); 3) specificity of the treatment plan to the problems that are presented (again depending oh the client's sex, sex-appropriateness of the problems, etc.); 4) the clinician's view of the client's prognosis (depending on client sex, etc).

## METHOD

### Subjects

Forty-five staff members (36 females) from alcohol treatment agencies in Nebraska participated in the study. Subjects, age 19 to 65 ($\bar{X}$ = 37) ranged in education from 12 to 17 years, with annual income between $7000 and $30,000, and were either engaged in front-line clinical service (86%) or clinical administration. Participants had come together for a statewide alcoholism training workshop during which the data were collected. As a group, subjects tended to endorse emergent rather than traditional sex-role values (82% of all values endorsed coming from the emergent end of the spectrum; see values card exercise described below).

## Procedure

Day one of the workshop focused on sex-role values clarification, examining the kinds of overtly stated values that may appeal to women seeking treatment, and exploring the effect of staff values on the comfort of their clients. Participants formed groups based on common values selected from the Values Options Process card deck developed by Mobley and Luciani.[8] The card deck contained 60 cards, half of which represent traditional sex-role values, the other half representing emergent values. Typical examples included bipolar items such as the following: "Children, even young ones, can be raised quite adequately by a father alone" (emergent); versus "Children, especially young ones, need a mother to care for them" (traditional). Subjects, each of whom were dealt three cards at random,* were asked to mill about the room discovering the values held by others, trading and discarding cards, and ultimately grouping with other participants with whom they shared the most important values.

After the groups were formed based on common values, each of the six groups that resulted was asked to take on the role of a "treatment center" stating its shared values to the community at large (the other "treatment centers"). Subjects were then asked to rate each treatment center on a 5-point scale to designate the degree of comfort they would feel with each agency if they were a client presenting themselves for treatment.

The second day of the workshop highlighted the differential perceptions of key problem areas in male and female clients. Subjects, first individually and then as a group, made up lists of "typical" male and female problems likely to be encountered in the alcoholic client. The three top male problems that emerged (job, legal, and family pressure) and the three top female problems (child care, financial, and no family support) were then assigned to male and female surrogate clients in a manner such that the three-item set of

---

*Two and a quarter decks were shuffled together.

problems could be either "sex-appropriate" or non "sex-ap-propriate." For client surrogates we used chairs designated as male or female by the attire that was draped over them. (Order effects were controlled for sex of client and sex of problem set; and order effect of individual problems was minimized by listing all problems in a triangular format rather than vertically or horizontally.)

Subjects were then assigned to "treatment teams" and asked to make a series of clinical assessments and treatment plans for two "clients" (a male and a female) who presented with the same set of stereotypically male or female problems. More specifically, subjects were asked to rate each client along a 5-point scale on each of the following dimensions: 1) *prognosis*—extent to which the client can be successfully treated; 2) *importance* of each of the client's three presenting problems; 3) *treatment plan*—services and supports that would be appropriate for dealing with each of the client's presenting problems. (A score representing specificity of treatment plan was computed for each problem based on the number of specific plans listed.) It should be noted that subjects did not know they would be rating the same set of problems for the male and female client (and generally did not realize that they had done so until the wrap up when they were asked to observe differences in the decisions and the assumptions that they had made based on the sex of the client). Confusion about the task was experimentally increased by presenting the problem list for the second client in a different handwriting.

## RESULTS

To determine the effect of treatment personnel's sex-role values on the comfort of surrogate clients seeking treatment, six correlations were computed between subjects' comfort ratings with each "treatment center" (values group) and the degree of disparity between the values of that treatment center and the subject's own values group. Five of the six correlations were significant ($p < .05$) with a mean correlation of .51—suggesting a substantial relationship between a client's comfort with a given agency and the degree of congruence between his/her sex-role values and the values of the treatment staff at that agency.

To examine the perceived importance of a client's presenting problems in relationship to: client sex, whether the problems presented are typically male or typically female problems, and sex-appropriateness of the problem, three two-way analyses of variance were computed. For the first analysis (sex of client by sex of presenting problems) importance ratings for each subject were pooled over the three problems that they were asked to rate. A significant Interaction Effect emerged (F = 16.36, p < .0005) indicating that sex-appropriate problems were seen as more important for both male and female clients than were non sex-appropriate problems. As can be seen from Table 1, stereotypically female problems are perceived as significantly more important when they occur in a female client than when they occur in a male. In addition, female problems in the male client are seen as significantly less important than male problems. (The opposite trend approaches significance

TABLE 1

MEAN IMPORTANCE RATINGS OF SEX-APPROPRIATE
AND NON SEX-APPROPRIATE PRESENTING PROBLEMS

|  | Male Client | Female Client |
|---|---|---|
| 'Male' Problem | 1.47 | 1.63 |
| 'Female' Problem | 1.82 | 1.42 |

[ = p < .05,  [ = p < .10; Low Score = more important

for male problems.) It is of some interest that the lowest importance of all is attached to female problems in a male client—a pattern that held up for the 9 male subjects in our sample as clearly as it did for the sample as a whole.

The two additional two-way designs (sex of clients by specific problem) examined first the data from subjects who rated the three male problems in both the female and male client, and then data from the subjects who rated the three female problems in both a male and female client. In both of these analyses the Interaction Effects were again significant ($F=5.70$, $p < .01$; $F=.3.70$, $p < .05$ respectively), indicating that the *same specific* problems take on different importance when viewed in a male as opposed to a female client. More specifically, (see Table 2) data from the analysis using the male set of problems showed that the problem "job" was considered significantly more important in a male client than in a female client, and in addition was seen as most important of all problems for the male but least important for the female. In contrast, for the female, "family pressure" was considered the most important problem (significantly more important than job problems) but was perceived to be the least important problem of all for male clients.

Looking at the data from the subjects who were assigned the female set of problems to rate, a similar picture emerges. The problem "child care" is seen as significantly more important in a female client than in a male and is also seen as the most important problem for the female client, while it is perceived as the least important problem for the male. In addition, a significant Main Effect for Sex emerges in this analysis, indicating that the problems of female clients overall were judged to be more important than the problems of male clients. (See Table 2b for Means.)

To examine specificity of treatment plans, three analyses of variance were computed parallel to those described above—first using a two-way repeated measures analysis that examined the data from all forty-five subjects but collapsed their scores over the specific problems rated, and then examining separately the data from those subjects who rated the three male problems in both the male and female client and those who rated the three female problems in both the male and female. The results of the first analysis were not significant. That is, no significant differences were found in treatment planning based on sex of client, whether the client presented with the male or the female set of problems, or the sex-appropriateness of

TABLE 2

MEAN IMPORTANCE RATINGS
OF PRESENTING PROBLEMS

a. Male Problem Set

| Problem | Sex of Client | |
|---|---|---|
| | Male | Female |
| Job | 1.26 | 1.84 |
| Legal | 1.53 | 1.68 |
| Family Pressure | 1.63 | 1.37 |

b. Female Problem Set

| Problem | Sex of Client | |
|---|---|---|
| | Male | Female |
| Child Care | 2.20 | 1.13 |
| No Family Support | 1.87 | 1.40 |
| Financial | 1.40 | 1.67 |
| | X = 1.82 | X = 1.40 |

[ = p < .05; Low Score = more important

the problems (i.e., the interaction). The second two analyses similarly failed to show either sex differences in specificity of treatment plan or differences in the plan based on whether a *given* problem appeared in a male as opposed to female client (i.e., the interaction). However, a significant Main Effect for specific problems emerge in both analyses (F=4.16, p < .05 and F=3.25, p < .10 for the analyses using the male and female problem sets, respectively), indicating that for both male and female clients, treatment plans tend

to be more specific for some problems than for others. (This was the .
case for family pressure in the male set and financial problems in the
female set.) See Table 3 for Means.

To examine the effect of client sex and sex-appropriateness of
presenting problems on judgments about prognosis, a single two-
way analysis of variance (client sex by sex of problems) was computed. The Main Effect for client sex was significant ($F=8.25$,
$p < .01$) indicating a poorer prognosis for female clients ($\overline{X}=2.23$)
than for males ($\overline{X}=2.57$) regardless of the nature of their presenting
problems. It is of some interest that this effect was contributed
almost entirely by the *female* subjects. Only 1 of the 9 male subjects
(11%) rated their female client surrogates as having a worse prognosis than their male client surrogates; in contrast, 13 of the 24*
female subjects (55%) rated their female clients as having a worse
prognosis than their male clients.

A final, unanticipated set of data bears comment, since it reflects
directly on the issue of sex bias. After forming groups based on
common values, each of the six groups was asked to choose a

TABLE 3

MEAN TREATMENT PLAN SPECIFICITY
SCORES FOR PRESENTING PROBLEMS

| a. Male Problem Set | | b. Female Problem Set | |
|---|---|---|---|
| Family Pressure | 2.08 | Financial | 2.47 |
| Job | 1.63 | No Family Support | 1.50 |
| Legal | 1.08 | Child Care | 1.31 |

[ = p < .05, [ = p < .10; High Score = greater specificity of plan

*Only 24 of the 36 women participants had complete data sets for inclusion in this
analysis.

spokesperson to share its values with the community at large. One-third (33 1/3%) of the men participating in the conference were selected to be spokespeople (3 men were selected of the 9 men participating), in contrast to only 8.3% of the women (3 women were selected of the 36 female participants). Thus, the male participants were 4 times more likely ( $X^2 = 4.29$, p < .05) to be selected as a spokesperson than were the women participants.

## DISCUSSION

The results of this study suggest that sex-role values of treatment personnel may influence a client's comfort in the clinical situation. More specifically, the data suggest that subjects (role playing clients) were more comfortable going to a treatment program that was perceived to hold values similar to their own than they were going to an agency that was perceived to hold discrepant values.

Our data also indicate that clinicians (in particular females) tend to see the female alcoholic as having a poorer prognosis than the male alcoholic. In addition, clinicians tend to perceive the presenting problems of both male and female clients to be more important if they are sex-appropriate than if they are not sex-appropriate. (The problems perceived as least important being "female" problems—in particular child care—in a male client.) No relationship was found between specificity of treatment planning and either the sex of the client or the sex-appropriateness of the client's presenting problems.

Our findings are consistent with a large body of research[9-11] documenting the fact that labels create sets that influence subsequent perceptions and judgments. Just as labeling a lecturer "warm" or "cold" has been found to influence raters' subsequent perceptions of him[9] or that children's behavior is viewed differently when raters are told the child is "feeling under par,"[11] in the present study clinicians' judgments about a surrogate client's prognosis and the importance of his/her problems differed depending on the sex ascribed to the patient. It is clear that the labels male and female carry meaning that significantly alters clinicians' judgments and expectations.

With regard to prognosis, it is important to note that there is no scientific basis for the belief that treated alcoholic women will do more poorly than treated alcoholic men.[12] However, this belief may itself be a factor in creating poor outcome. Reams of work on experimentor bias suggest that clinicians' expectations may have considerable influence on clinical judgment, perceptions of behavior, and on actual treatment outcome. Leake and King's[13] study with alcoholic clients is of particular interest in this regard. In a carefully designed expectancy study, counselors were falsely led to believe at the beginning of the detox period that certain of their clients could be expected to show "a remarkable recovery" during the course of counseling. At follow-up, on a number of job and drinking-related outcome measures, patients randomly assigned to the high expectancy condition (where therapists were given positive expectations) performed significantly better than control subjects. Although the Leake and King study did not experimentally produce negative expectancies (only positive and neutral expectancies) it is instructive in highlighting the possible consequences of negative expectancies that therapists may consciously or unconsciously transmit.

Of some concern in this project was the fact that we were collecting data regarding sex-role stereotyping from subjects who had come together knowing that they would be exploring this issue. It was our concern, in particular, that the heightened sensitivity would minimize any experimental effects since we expected that subjects would be trying *not* to be biased. We were especially worried because such a workshop tends to non-randomly select participants—collecting more individuals from the liberated portion of the sex-role ideology spectrum. (This was validated by our own data showing that as a whole our group tended to endorse emergent rather than traditional values.)

In fact, the neutralizing effects were less than we had expected—and some interesting surprises also occurred. In particular, although there were only nine males at the conference (thirty-six females), three of the six values groups that were formed chose a male member as the spokesperson to share its values with the community at large. It appears that even when men are clearly in the minority in a group of presumably sensitized people, sex-role values prevail and have a striking impact. This also occurred in the listing of problem areas for male and female clients: "job" was not listed among important problems for women—though, of course, *all* of the women in our subject sample worked! Finally, we noted with amusement that the treatment plan prepared for one male "client" with child care as one of the presenting problems included the comment, "How come he got dumped with the kids?" This suggested a real loss of distance and perspective, even in a group of subjects who knew the general set of the training program. In the end, we were impressed with the pervasiveness of sex-role bias and the insidiousness with which this bias invades our decision making processes.

Before concluding, a word is in order about the generalizability of our findings. This was, in effect, a study of a roleplaying situation in which alcohol treatment personnel were asked first to play the role of clients, and later, of therapists. It thus raises the question whether subjects acting as clients respond in the way they would in a real clinical situation and similarly, whether subjects making therapeutic decisions in an analog situation make the same kinds of decisions as in a real clinical situation. Such questions of generalizability are appropriately raised in any analog study. However, the fact that in real life our subjects did work as health care professionals (mostly front line) and that many had no doubt been clients seeking treatment at earlier points in their careers we feel lends weight to the validity of our findings and to their implications for actual clinical practice.

# REFERENCES

1. Rubin, J.Z., Provenzano, F.J., and Luria, Z. The eye of the beholder: Parents' views on sex of newborns. Am J Orthopsychiatry. 1974, 44: 512-519.

2. Levine, S.V., Kamin. L.E., and Levine, E.L. Sexism and psychiatry. Am J Orthopsychiatry. 1973, 44(3): 327-334.

3. Abramowitz. S., Abramowitz, C., Jackson, C., and Gomes. B. The politics of clinical judgment: What nonliberal examiners infer about women who do not stifle themselves. J Consult Clin Psychol. 1973, 41: 385-391.

4. Broverman, I.K., Broverman, D.M., Clarkson, F.E., Rosenkrantz, P., and Vogel, S.R. Sex-role stereotypes and clinical judgments of mental health. J Consult and Clin Psychol. 1970, 34: 1-7.

5. Broverman, I.K., Vogel, S.R., Broverman, D.M., Clarkson, F.E., and Rosenkrantz, P.S. Sex-role stereotypes: A current appraisal. J Social Issues. 1972, 28(2): 58-78.

6. Fabrikant, B. The psychotherapist and the female patient: Perceptions and change. In V. Franks and V. Burtle (Eds.), Women in therapy. New York: Brunner/Mazel, 1974.

7. Lerner, H. Adaptive and pathogenic aspects of sex-role stereotypes: Implications for parenting and psychotherapy. Am J Psychiatry. 1978, 135: 48-52.

8. Mobley, and Luciani. Values Options Process Cards. Mobley, Luciani Associates, Inc. 1975.

9. Kelly, H.H. The warm-cold variable in first impressions of persons. J Personality. 1950, 18: 431-439.

10. Langer, E.J., and Abelson, R.P. A patient by any other name. . . : Clinician group difference in labeling bias. J Consult Clin Psychol. 1974, 42(1): 4-9.

11. Rapp, D.W. 1965. Detection of observer bias in the written record. Unpublished manuscript, University of Georgia. Cited in R. Rosenthal, Experimenter Effects in Behavioral Research. New York: Appleton-Century Crofts, 1966: 21.

12. Vannicelli, M. Treatment outcome of alcoholic women: The state of the art in relation to sex bias and expectancy effects. In Alcohol Problems in Women: Antecedents, Causes, and Interventions. Wilsnack, S. and Beckman, L. (Ed.) Guilford Press. In Press.

13. Leake, G.J., & King, A.G. Effect of counselor expectations on alcoholic recovery. Alcohol Health and Research World. 1(3): 16-22, 1977.

# SELECTIVE GUIDE
# TO CURRENT REFERENCE SOURCES
# ON TOPICS DISCUSSED
# IN THIS ISSUE

## Cultural and Sociological Aspects
## of Alcoholism and Substance Abuse

Theodora Andrews

Each issue of *Advances in Alcohol & Substance Abuse* will feature a section offering suggestions on where to look for further information on that issue's theme. Our intent is to guide readers to sources which will provide substantial information on the specific theme presented, rather than on the entire field of alcohol and substance abuse. We aim to be selective, not comprehensive, and in most cases we shall emphasize current rather than retrospective material.

Some reference sources utilize designated terminology (controlled vocabularies) which must be used to find material on topics of interest. For these we shall indicate a sample of available search terms so that the reader can assess the suitability of sources for his/her purposes. Other reference tools use key words or free text terms (generally from the title of the document, agency, or meeting listed). In searching the latter the user should look under all synonyms for the concept in question.

Theodora Andrews is Professor of Library Science; Pharmacy, Nursing, and Health Sciences Librarian, Purdue University, W. Lafayette, IN 47907.

69

Readers are encouraged to consult with their librarians for further assistance before undertaking research on a topic.

Suggestions regarding the content and organization of this section will be welcomed.

## 1a. INDEXING AND ABSTRACTING TOOLS

*Dissertation Abstracts International. A., Humanities and Social Sciences.* Ann Arbor, MI, University Microfilms International, 1938– , monthly.
> Since 1970 (vol. 30) keyword title indexing has been provided as well as author.

*Excerpta Medica: Drug Dependence. Section 40.* Amsterdam, The Netherlands, Excerpta Medica, 1972– , monthly.
> Search terms: Alcohol; Alcoholism (and listing beneath); Ethnic group, Youth; and names of drugs.

*Excerpta Medica: Public Health, Social Medicine, and Hygiene. Section 17.* Amsterdam, The Netherlands, Excerpta Medica, 1955– , 20 times per year.
> Search terms: Addiction; Drug dependence; Drug abuse; Alcoholism; Ethnic group.

*Index Medicus* (including *Bibliography of Medical Reviews*). Bethesda, MD, National Library of Medicine, 1960– , monthly.
> Indexing terms are called *MeSH* terms. See: Substance abuse; Substance dependence; Substance use disorders; Alcoholism; Psychosocial deprivation; Socal problems; Ethnic group; and also names of drugs.
> NOTE: Indexing terms for the *Bibliography of Medical Reviews* are similar, except broader terms are used to enable grouping of similar material.

*Psychological Abstracts.* Washington, DC, American Psychological Association, 1927– , monthly.
> Search terms: Drug abuse; Drug dependency; Drug addiction; Alcohol drinking attitudes; Alcoholism.

*Psychopharmacology Abstracts.* Rockville, MD, National Institute of Mental Health, 1961– , quarterly.
> Indexed by keywords from specific words appearing in titles. See: Alcohol; Alcoholism; Drug-dependence; Women.

*Public Affairs Information Service. Bulletin.* New York, Public Affairs Information Service, 1915– , semi-monthly.

Search terms: Alcoholism; Drug abuse; Drug addicts; Women —Drug problems.

*Social Sciences Citation Index.* Philadelphia, Institute for Scientific Information, 1973- , 3 times per year.

Usually searched through citations, but has a "Permuterm Subject Index" generated from title words of source items indexed in the publication. To use the citation index look up name of author known to have published material relevant to the subject area of interest. Cited authors will be listed. Then use source index for complete description of articles found through the citation index.

*Social Sciences Index.* New York, H. W. Wilson Co., 1974- , quarterly.

Search terms: Drug abuse; Drug addicts; Alcoholism; Drugs and women; Drugs and youth; Drugs and blacks; Alcohol drinking behavior; Indians of North America—alcoholism.

*Social Work Research and Abstracts.* New York, National Association of Social Workers, 1965- , quarterly.

Search terms: Alcoholism; Addicts; Drug abuse; Drug addicts.

*Sociological Abstracts.* San Diego, CA, International Sociological Association, 1953- , 5 times per year.

Search terms: Addict/addicts/addicted/addictive/addiction; Drug addict/drug addiction; Drug/drugs; Alcoholic/alcoholics /alcoholism; Drinking/drinkers.

1b. ON-LINE BIBLIOGRAPHIC DATA BASES (Consult a librarian for search formulation.)

*BOOKS IN PRINT* (data base)

Contains bibliographic information on virtually the entire U.S. book publishing output. Includes: *A Subject Guide to Books in Print; Forthcoming Books; Scientific and Technical Books in Print;* and *Medical Books in Print.*

*BOOKSINFO (BOOK)*

Contains citations to more than 600,000 English language monographs currently in print from approximately 10,000 U.S. publishers (including academic and small presses) and 200 foreign publishers.

*CONFERENCE PAPERS INDEX*

Provides access to records of more than 100,000 scientific and technical papers presented at over 1,000 major regional, national, and international meetings each year. A guide, *Conference Papers User Index Guide,* is available.

DISSERTATION ABSTRACTS ON-LINE

Former name of this data base was *Comprehensive Dissertation Index.* It is a subject, title, and author guide to American dissertations accepted at accredited institutions. Contents correspond to *Dissertation Abstracts International, American Doctoral Dissertations, Comprehensive Disseration Index,* and *Master Abstracts.* Beginning in January 1984 abstracts were added to the file for the years 1980-present. These abstracts are about 350 words in length and describe the original research project upon which the disseration is based.

DRUGINFO-ALCOHOL USE/ABUSE

Contains citations from two different agencies: Druginfo Service Center of the College of Pharmacy of the University of Minnesota, and the Hazelden Foundation.

EMBASE (formerly *EXCERPTA MEDICA)*

Search terms are those used in the printed index sections, but everything is combined rather than treated in sections. There are over two million records in the base. See: Excerpta Medica's *Guide to the Excerpta Medica Classification and Indexing System.*

FOUNDATION DIRECTORY (Copyright Foundation Center)

Is indexed by fields of interest. Provides descriptions of more than 3,500 foundations which have assets of $1 million or more or which make grants of $100,000 or more annually.

FOUNDATION GRANTS INDEX (Copyright Foundation Center)

Subject access available. Contains information on grants awarded by more than 400 major American philanthropic foundations representing all records from the "Foundation Grants Index" section of the bimonthly *Foundation News.*

GOP (*Government Printing Office) MONTHLY CATALOG*

This is the machine-readable equivalent of the printed *Monthly Catalog of United States Government Publications.*

GRANTS DATABASE

Provides subject access to information on currently available grants. Produced by Oryx Press. Includes information on 2,200 grants offered by federal, state, and local governments, commercial organizations, associations, and private foundations.

MEDLINE (Medical Literature Analysis Retrieval System On-Line)

Search terms are those used in the printed *Index Medicus* (MeSH).

**MENTAL HEALTH ABSTRACTS**
All areas of mental health are covered from 1969-present. There is no equivalent printed publication.

**NATIONAL FOUNDATIONS** (Copyright Foundation Center)
Indexed by activity code. Covers the current year. Provides records of all 21,800 U.S. foundations which award grants regardless of the assets of the foundation or the total amount of grants it awards annually.

**NTIS** (National Technical Information Service)
This data base consists of government-sponsored research, development, and engineering reports as well as other analysis prepared by government agencies, their contractors, or grantees. An increasing proportion of the data base consists of unpublished material originating from outside the U.S. Several thesauri are used since material comes from a number of government agencies.

**PAIS INTERNATIONAL**
Corresponds to *Public Affairs Information Service Bulletin.* Contains references to information in all fields of social sciences.

**PRE-MED (PREM)**
Contains citations indexed previous to their appearance in MEDLINE. Search terms are those used in *Index Medicus* (MeSH).

**PRE-PSYCH**
Begins with journals published in the fall of 1981. Citations appear within 4-8 weeks of their publication. Covers clinical psychology from 98 core psychological journals, and also psychological literature as it relates to criminal justice, the family, and education.

**PSYCHINFO**
Corresponds to the printed publication, *Psychological Abstracts.*

**SOCIAL SCISEARCH**
Indexed like the printed sources *(Social Sciences Citation Index* and *Current Contents: Social and Behavioral Sciences)* that is, keywords from titles.

**SOCIOLOGICAL ABSTRACTS**
Corresponds to the printed index.

## 1c. BIBLIOGRAPHY OF BIBLIOGRAPHIES

*Bibliographic Index.* Bronx, NY, H. W. Wilson Co., 1937– , 3 times per year.
> Drug abuse; Youth, drug use; Medication abuse; Women, drug use; Indians of North America, alcohol use; Alcoholism; Alcoholics.

## 1d. CURRENT AWARENESS PUBLICATIONS

*Current Contents: Clinical Practice.* Philadelphia, Institute for Scientific Information, 1973– , weekly.
> Indexed by keywords from titles, examples: Alcohol; Alcoholism; Alcoholics; Drug abuse; Addiction; Addicts.

*Current Contents: Social and Behavioral Sciences.* Philadelphia, Institute for Scientific Information, 1969– , weekly.
> Indexed by keywords from titles, examples: Alcohol; Alcohol abuse; Alcoholics; Alcoholism; Addicts; Drug use.

## 2. SOURCES OF NOTICES OF BOOKS, PERIODICALS, AND OTHER PUBLICATIONS

Andrews, Theodora, *A Bibliography of Drug Abuse, including Alcohol and Tobacco.* Littleton, CO, Libraries Unlimited, Inc., 1977.

Andrews, Theodora, *A Bibliography of Drug Abuse, Supplement 1977-1980.* Littleton, CO, Libraries Unlimited, Inc., 1981.

Bemko, Jane. *Substance Abuse Book Review Index.* Toronto, Addiction Research Foundation, 1980– , annual.
> Begins with 1978 material. Does not contain actual reviews, but guides the user to journals that have reviewed publications in the drug abuse field.

*Books in Print.* New York, R. R. Bowker Co. Several volumes. Annual. Supplements issued periodically.
> Author and title listings.

*Critiques.* Madison, WI, Wisconsin Clearinghouse of Alcohol and Other Drug Information, 1979– , bimonthly.
> A review periodical that publishes evaluations of new films, books, and pamphlets in the substance abuse field.

*Forthcoming Books.* New York, R. R. Bowker Co. 6 times per year.

*Irregular Serials and Annuals, 1984: An International Directory.*
9th ed. New York, R. R. Bowker Co., 1983.
>Arranged by broad subjects, e.g., Drug abuse, and Alcoholism.

*National Library of Medicine Current Catalog.* Bethesda, MD,
U.S. National Library of Medicine, 1966– , quarterly.
>Search terms are the same as those used in *Index Medicus* (MeSH)

*Subject Guide to Books in Print.* New York, R. R. Bowker Co. Several volumes. Annual.

*Ulrich's International Periodicals Directory.* 22nd ed. Vol.1-2.
New York, R. R. Bowker Co., 1983.
>Arranged by broad subjects, e.g., Drug abuse, and Alcoholism.

NOTE: Many journals of the field include reviews of recent books.
See also in Section 1b, on-line bibliographic data bases BOOKS IN
PRINT and BOOKSINFO.

## 3. U.S. GOVERNMENT PUBLICATIONS

*Government Reports Announcements and Index.* Springfield, VA,
National Technical Information Service. Biweekly.
>Contains a biological and medical sciences section, further subdivided. Has a keyword index of words selected from a controlled vocabulary of terms. Examples: Alcoholism; Alcoholic beverages.

*Monthly Catalog of United States Government Publications.* Washington, DC, U.S. Government Printing Office. Monthly.
>Has a subject index and also can be approached through key words in titles.
>Search terms: Alcoholism (and also subdivisions); Drug abuse.

## 4. SOURCES OF INFORMATION ON GRANTS

*Annual Register of Grant Support.* Chicago, Marquis Academic Media. Annual.
>Has indexes by subject, organization and program, geographic area and personnel.

*Foundation Grants Index.* Edited by Lee Noe et al. New York,
Foundation Center. Annual.
>Has a subject index.

*Fund Sources in Health and Allied Fields.* Compiled by William K.
  Wilson and Betty L. Wilson. Phoenix, Oryx Press. Monthly.
    A newsletter of interest to professionals who need to know what
    fund sources are available. Government and foundation grants
    both are included.
*NIH Guide for Grants and Contracts.* Washington, DC, U.S. De-
  partment of Health and Human Services.
    Published at irregular intervals to announce scientific initiatives
    and to provide policy and administrative information to in-
    dividuals and organizations who need to be kept informed of
    opportunities, requirements, and changes in grants and con-
    tracts activities administered by the National Institutes of
    Health.
See also in Section 1b, on-line bibliographic data bases FOUNDA-
  TION DIRECTORY,
    FOUNDATION GRANTS INDEX, GRANTS DATABASE
    and NATIONAL FOUNDATIONS. In addition, see Raper,
    James E., Jr. et al., "Grantsmanship, Granting Agencies and
    Future Prospects for Grant Support" in *Advances in Alcohol
    and Substance Abuse,* vol. 2 no. 3, Spring, 1983, p.71-79.

## 5. GUIDES TO UPCOMING MEETINGS

*World Meetings: Medicine.* New York, Macmillan Publishing Co.
  Quarterly.
    See Keyword subject index, sponsor directory and index.

## 6. PROCEEDING OF MEETINGS

*Conference Papers Index.* Louisville, KY, Data Courier, Inc.,
  1973- , monthly.
*Directory of Published Proceedings, Series SEMT - Science, Engi-
  neering, Medicine and Technology.* Harrison, NY, InterDok
  Corp., 1965- , 10 times per year.
    Principal indexing is by key word in the name of the conference
    and the titles. Also has a sponsor index.
*Directory of Published Proceedings, Series SSH - Social Sciences/
  Humanities.* Harrison, NY, InterDok Corp., 1968- , quarterly.
*Index of Conference Proceedings Received.* The British Library,
  Lending Division, 1964- , monthly with annual, 5 and 10 year
  cumulations.
    Search terms: Addiction; Drug abuse; Addictive drugs; Drug

dependence; Alcohol; Alcohol abuse; Alcohol studies; Alcoholism.

*Proceedings in Print.* Arlington, MA, Proceedings in Print, Inc., 1964– , bimonthly.
Covers all subject areas and all languages.

## 7. MISCELLANEOUS RELEVANT PUBLICATIONS
NOTE: Some of the publications in this section are guides of information on the topic under review; others provide relevant information directly.

*Alcoholism and Alcohol Abuse among Women: Research Issues.* Proceedings of a workshop, April 2-5, 1978. Jekyll Island, GA, sponsored by the Division of Extramural Research, U.S. National Institute on Alcohol Abuse and Alcoholism. (NIAAA Research Monograph No. 1; DHEW Publication No. ADM 80-835). Washington, DC, U.S. Government Printing Office, 1980.
Of value to the alcohol researcher in that it represents the major thinking prior to 1978.

Austin, Gregory A., and Michael L. Prendergast. *Drug Use and Abuse: A Guide to Research Findings.* Vol.1: *Adults.* Vol.2: *Adolescents.* Santa Barbara, CA, ABC-Clio Information Services, 1984.
Provides an assessment of and digests research carried out from about 1970-1980. The abstracts are arranged by topic within a number of categories, including: drug use among women, among ethnic minorities, and among students.

Blane, Howard T., and Morris E. Chafetz, eds. *Youth, Alcohol, and Social Policy.* New York, Plenum Press, 1979.
Papers from a conference organized by the Health Education Foundation which was held October 18-20, 1978 in Arlington, VA. Provides recent information on the epidemiology of drinking behavior and drinking problems among the young, theories that may explain drinking behavior, social policy implications youthful drinking, and a review of programs designed to reduced problems associated with alcohol.

Blum, Richard H., and Associates. *Horatio Alger's Children: the Role of the Family in the Origin and Prevention of Drug Risk.* San Francisco, CA, Jossey-Bass, Inc., 1972.
Findings of the study show that drug use among the young can be predicted by examining certain characteristics of the fam-

ily. The key factors were found to be social class, religion, drinking habits, medical practices, and attitudes toward authority.

Bowker, Lee H. *Drug Use Among American Women, Old and Young: Sexual Oppression and Other Themes.* San Francisco, CA, R & E Research Associates, 1977.
    Focuses on the interaction of women's studies and female drug abuse. Literature of the field was examined and a large bibliography included.

Brake, Mike. *The Sociology of Youth Culture and Youth Subcultures: Sex and Drugs and Rock'n'roll?* London, Boston, Routledge & Kegan Paul, 1980.
    The author examines research done on youth culture, subcultures, and delinquency covering the early thirties until recently in both Great Britain and the U.S.

Camberwell Council on Alcoholism. *Women and Alcohol.* London, Tavistock Publications, 1980. (Available in the U.S. from Methuen, Inc., New York.)

Corrigan, Eileen M. *Alcoholic Women in Treatment.* New York, Oxford University Press, 1980.
    Covers patterns of drinking; consequences of drinking; marriages, children and husbands; family etiology of alcholism; and outcomes of treatment.

Cuskey, Walter R., and Richard B. Wathey. *Female Addiction: A Longitudinal Study.* Lexington, MA, Lexington Books, 1982.

Dawkins, Marvin P. *Alcohol and the Black Community: Exploratory Studies of Selected Issues.* Saratoga, CA, Century Twenty-One, 1980.
    Covers research, social, and policy issues.

Eddy, Cristen C., and John L. Ford, eds. *Alcoholism in Women.* Dubuque, IA, Kendall Hunt Pub. Co., 1980. (Topics in Human Behavior Series.)
    Contains articles with references on etiological factors, primary and secondary prevention, and treatment.

Edwards, Griffith, and Awni Arif, eds. *Drug Problems in the Sociocultural Context: A Basis for Policies and Programme Planning.* Geneva, World Health Organization, 1980. (Public Health Papers, No. 73.)

Greeley, Andrew M., William C. McCready, and Gary Theisen. *Ethnic Drinking Subcultures.* Brooklyn, NY, J. F. Bergin Publishers (Praeger), 1980.

An examination of the use of alcohol, ethnic diversity, and socialization among five religioethnic groups in the U.S., the Irish, Jewish, Italians, Swedish, and the English (as a control group).

Hamer, John, and Jack Steinbring, eds. *Alcohol and Native Peoples of the North.* Lanham, MD, University Press of America, 1980.

Heath, Dwight B., Jack O. Waddell, and Martin Topper, eds. *Cultural Factors in Alcohol Research and Treatment of Drinking Problems.* Published in cooperation with the Smithsonian Institution. Piscataway, NJ, Center of Alcoholic Studies, 1981. (Journal of Studies on Alcohol, Supplement No. 9, January 1981.)

Helmer, John. *Drugs and Minority Oppression.* New York, Seabury Press, 1975. (A Continuum Book.)

Hornik, Edith Lynn. *The Drinking Woman.* New York, Association Press, 1977.

Alcoholism is described, then life situations women encounter discussed, such as pregnancy, stress, family life, feminism, and sexuality. There are chapters on special groups such as black women, Jewish women, American Indians, Eskimos, and senior citizens.

Kalant, Oriana Josseau, ed. *Alcohol and Drug Problems in Women.* New York, Plenum Press, 1980. (Research Advances in Alcohol and Drug Problems, v.5.)

The central point is that drug and alcohol use and abuse are different for women than for men.

Kane, Geoffrey P. *Inner-City Alcoholism: An Ecological Analysis and Cross-Cultural Study.* New York, Human Sciences Press, 1981.

A descriptive epidemiologic study of 372 black and Hispanic alcoholics in the South Bronx section of New York City.

Maddox, George L., ed. *The Domesticated Drug: Drinking among Collegians.* New Haven, CT, College and University Press, 1970.

Attempts to present a balanced view of drinking among American college students.

Malikin, David. *Social Disability; Alcoholism, Drug Addiction, Crime and Social Disadvantage.* New York, New York University Press, 1973.

Includes four case histories and a review of the literature, which is mainly from the fields of psychology, social work, and rehabilitation.

O'Connor, Joyce. *The Young Drinkers: A Cross-National Study of Social and Cultural Influences.* London, Tavistock Publications, 1978.

The following matters are focused upon: parental influences, peer group influences, social and personal influences, and ethnic and cultural influences.

Ralston, Edward J. *Family Structures of Drug Abusers.* Monticello, IL, Vance Bibliographies, 1980. (Public Administration Series: Bibliography; P-557.)

*Sexological Aspects of Substance Use and Abuse.* Special issue of *Journal of Psychoactive Drugs,* Vol. 14, nos. 1-2, Jan.-June, 1982.

Stanton, M. Duncan, Thomas C. Todd, and Associates. *The Family Therapy of Drug Abuse and Addiction.* New York, Guilford Publications, 1982.

Identifies maladaptive patterns occurring in families of drug abusers and offers strategies for altering and restructuring these patterns.

U.S. National Institute on Drug Abuse. *Drug Abuse Patterns Among Young Polydrug Users and Urban Appalachian Youths.* Washington, DC, GPO, 1980. (DHHS Publication No. ADM 80-1102; NIDA Services Research Report.)

Two reports are presented here. Both report findings on the nature and patterns of drug use among the young. Findings indicate that one should anticipate varying patterns of drug use among the young, and programs serving them should take account of the youths' family and school relationships.

U.S. National Institute on Drug Abuse. *Drugs and Minorities.* Edited by Gregory A. Austin, et al. Washington, DC, GPO, 1977. (DHEW Publication No. ADM 78-507; NIDA Research Issues No. 21.)

Summarizes research that focuses on the extent of drug abuse among racial and ethnic minorities and the factors influencing it.

Waddell, Jack O., and Michael W. Everett, eds. *Drinking Behavior Among Southwestern Indians: An Anthropological Perspective.* Tucson, AZ, University of Arizona Press, 1980.

The authors deal with a spectrum of drinking styles. Most of the contributors emphasize that heavy drinking is considered a "way of life" by many Indians, rather than abnormal behavior.

# 8. SPECIAL LIBRARIES WITH COLLECTIONS OF NOTE

Alcoholism and Drug Addiction Research Foundation Library, 33 Russell St., Toronto, Ontario M5S 2S1, Canada

Rutgers University Center of Alcohol Studies Library, Smithers Hall, Busch Campus, New Brunswick, NJ 08903.

# Information for Authors

*Advances in Alcohol & Substance Abuse* publishes original articles and topical review articles related to all areas of substance abuse. Each publication will be issue-oriented and may contain both basic science and clinical papers.

All submitted manuscripts are read by the editors. Many manuscripts may be further reviewed by consultants. Comments from reviewers will be returned with the rejected manuscripts when it is believed that this may be helpful to the author(s).

The editor reserves the right to make those revisions necessary to achieve maximum clarity and conciseness as well as uniformity to style. *Advances in Alcohol & Substance Abuse* accepts no responsibility for statements made by contributing author(s).

## *MANUSCRIPT PREPARATION*

A double-spaced original and two copies (including references, legends, and footnotes) should be submitted. The manuscript should have margins of at least 4 cm, with subheadings used at appropriate intervals to aid in presentation. There is no definite limitation on length, although a range of fifteen to twenty typed pages is desired.

A cover letter should accompany the manuscript containing the name, address, and phone number of the individual who will be specifically responsible for correspondence.

### *Title Page*

The first page should include title, subtitle (if any), first name, and last name of each author, with the highest academic degree obtained. Each author's academic and program affiliation(s) should be noted, including the name of the department(s) and institution(s) to which the work should be attributed; disclaimers (if any); and the name and address of the author to whom reprint requests should be addressed. Any acknowledgements of financial support should also be listed.

### *Abstracts*

The second page should contain an abstract of not more than 150 words.

## References

References should be typed double space on separate pages and arranged according to their order in the text. In the text the references should be in superscript arabic numerals. The form of references should conform to the Index Medicus (National Library of Medicine) style. Sample references are illustrated below:

1. Brown MJ, Salmon D, Rendell M. Clonidine hallucinations. Ann Intern Med. 1980; 93:456-7.
2. Friedman HJ, Lester D. A critical review of progress towards an animal model of alcoholism. In: Blum K, ed. Alcohol and opiates: neurochemical and behavioral mechanisms. New York: Academic Press, 1977:1-19.
3. Berne E. Principles of group treatment. New York: Oxford University Press, 1966.

Reference to articles in press must state name of journal and, if possible, volume and year. References to unpublished material should be so indicated in parentheses in the text.

It is the responsibility of the author(s) to check references against the original source for accuracy both in manuscript and in galley proofs.

## Tables and Figures

Tables and figures should be unquestionably clear so that their meaning is understandable without the text. Tables should be typed double space on separate sheets with number and title. Symbols for units should be confined to column headings. Internal, horizontal, and vertical lines may be omitted. The following footnote symbols should be used:* † ‡ § ¶

Figures should be submitted as glossy print photos, untrimmed and unmounted. The label pasted on the back of each illustration should contain the name(s) of author(s) and figure number, with top of figure being so indicated. Photomicrographs should have internal scale markers, with the original magnification as well as stain being used noted. If figures are of patients, the identities should be masked or a copy of permission for publication included. If the figure has been previously published, permission must be obtained from the previous author(s) and copyright holder(s). Color illustrations cannot be published.

Manuscripts and other communications should be addressed to:

Barry Stimmel, MD
Mount Sinai School of Medicine
One Gustave L. Levy Place
Annenberg 5-12
New York, New York 10029